(1/23)

Life Lessons

Fifty Things I Learned in My First Fifty Years

Patrick Madrid

Ignatius Press–Augustine Institute

San Francisco   Greenwood Village, CO

Ignatius Press Distribution
P.O. Box 1339
Fort Collins, CO 80522
Tel: (800) 651-1531
www.ignatius.com

Augustine Institute
6160 S. Syracuse Way, Suite 310
Greenwood Village, CO 80111
Tel: (866) 767-3155
www.augustineinstitute.org

Cover Design: Christopher Murphy

Contents

Preface

"Someday, you'll understand" is an admonition I've heard countless times over the years. Unfortunately, when I was younger and dumber or in too much of a hurry to get on with my life, I paid this concept scant attention.

I wish I had listened. I wish I had paid attention when people who had been on this planet a lot longer than me—men and women who had traveled farther down the highway of life than I had or who'd been dinged up pretty bad by adversity, affliction, or their own bad decisions—bothered to try and help me with a kind (or sometimes harsh) word of advice.

"Yeah, well, someday is a long way away," I'd often think to myself. "I've got *all* the time in the world." Well, life doesn't work that way, I eventually discovered. You see, as anyone with enough gray in his hair will tell you, time marches on. Time waits for no man. Time is of the essence. Time keeps on slippin', slippin', slippin' into the future, as someone once put it.

All of which means that there's no time like the present to learn a good lesson. Or a few. Or *fifty* of them, as the case may be. I wrote this book as a kind of monument to all the times I've said to myself, sometimes wistfully, sometimes ruefully, "If only I knew then what I know now."

Perhaps something shared in these pages will be useful to you and maybe even save you some time and trouble or heartache. That's my sincere prayer.

Anyone who's lived more than fifty years (I'll turn fifty-six soon) has surely learned far more than fifty important lessons, as is true for me. And, as you might expect, some of my life's lessons aren't appropriate for sharing here, not because they weren't meaningful or life-changing, but because I'm not nearly as brave as St. Augustine was when he wrote his classic autobiography, *The Confessions,* and let it all hang out. So, I've passed over in a discrete silence some of life's more distinctive pitfalls and entanglements that I've lived to tell about but that I have chosen to tell only to God and my confessor. That is as it should be, I believe. Something true for all of us, in the mercy and grace of God's loving providence.

Here's a bonus lesson before you get started:

> God loves you just the way you are, but he loves you too much to let you stay that way.

If that little thought doesn't hit home right now, if it doesn't kind of bonk you on the head and shake you up a little, don't worry. Eventually, it will. Someday, you'll understand.

Patrick Madrid, 1966

Chapter 1

Guilt Show

SOME YEARS ago, as I pulled my rental car into the parking lot of the Catholic parish where I would be giving a lecture that evening, I glanced up at the large, new non-denominational Protestant church standing prominently on a nearby hill. What caught my eye was a large banner stretched across its facade that read in big, bold letters: GUILT SHOW.

"*Guilt* show? What's a guilt show?" I asked myself, puzzled by the enigmatic message. It didn't take long, though, before I had figured it out. Those Protestants up there on that hill were mocking Catholics, I reasoned indignantly. The folks who attend this parish have to see that banner every time they come to Mass. Why else would it be so prominently displayed?

"Guilt show" must obviously express those people's disdain for the Catholic Sacrament of Penance. After all, those Protestants believe in the doctrine of eternal security: once saved, always saved. In other words, that "true Christians" cannot lose their salvation. They regard the Catholic emphasis on guilt, examining one's conscience, and confession to be wrong and unbiblical. So I was certain that that's what the banner meant. Clearly, those Protestants up on the hill were mocking Catholics!

I asked the parish secretary what she thought it meant. "Oh, I never really noticed it," she said. But when I explained what *I* thought it meant a look of dismay crossed her face. It had never occurred to her that the next-door neighbors up the hill might be making fun of her and her fellow Catholics.

I decided to take the bull by the horns and call the Protestant church to ask them directly about the banner.

"Hi, I'm from out of town," I told the friendly receptionist who answered the phone, "and I am curious about the banner you have out front. What does 'guilt show' mean? Is it intended to be some kind of message for Catholics?"

"Guilt show?" she asked, befuddled by my question. She paused for a moment and then said, "Oh, you mean the *Quilt* Show banner," she chuckled. "Yes, we're hosting a quilt show here next weekend and everyone's invited."

Boy, did I feel stupid.

Sheepishly, I explained that the banner must have been folded a little—just enough to make the Q in "quilt" look like a G as in "guilt." She said she'd have the janitor smooth it out so it would read properly.

I thanked her and hung up, ashamed of myself for having so quickly jumped to the (totally erroneous) conclusion that "those Protestants" up on their hill were taunting Catholics. In my haste to account for the banner I had assumed ill will on their part, concluding without any evidence that their motives were dishonorable.

I had done, albeit in a minor way, exactly what Jesus tells us not to do:

> "Judge not, that you be not judged. For with the judgment you pronounce you will be judged, and the measure you give will be the measure you get. Why do you see the speck that is in your brother's eye, but do not notice the log that is in your own eye?

Or how can you say to your brother, 'Let me take the speck out of your eye,' when there is the log in your own eye? You hypocrite, first take the log out of your own eye, and then you will see clearly to take the speck out of your brother's eye." (Mt 7:1–5)

The memory of that incident has never left me. Many times since, when I have been tempted to assume the worst of others based solely on appearances, or impute bad motives to someone who disagrees with me, or judge other people's hearts, I've thought of that banner.

Maybe God intended it to read GUILT SHOW just for me. After all, it showed me I had something in my eye.

———————————◆———————————

"Do not judge by appearances, but judge with right judgment" (Jn 7:24).

Chapter 2

The Beggar

ONE EVENING, on my commute home from a long day at the office, I stopped at a gas station/mini-market to refuel and grab a cup of coffee. As I got to the entrance, a bedraggled young man of about twenty stepped nervously toward me from the shadows.

"Please, sir . . ." he said in a low, faltering voice. We locked eyes for an instant. I sized him up before glancing away with a grimace of irritation. He seemed kind of scared, as if he were about to cry. Ashamed of begging, perhaps.

"Please, sir . . . I'm . . ."

"Sorry," I cut him off, raising my hand dismissively as I walked past. Once inside, I poured myself a steaming cup of freshly brewed coffee, tossed a $50 bill on the counter, and told the clerk, "I'll have this coffee and give me the rest on pump seven."

I headed back out, sipping my coffee and thinking, *I hope that beggar is gone by now.*

No such luck. There he was, standing silently in the same place as before. I strode by, pretending not to see him.

I pumped the gas, got back in my car, and drove out of the parking lot, coffee in hand, as I thought about how nice it would be to get home to my easy chair and a glass of wine and the delicious dinner my wife had cooked for me.

That's when an explosion of remorse burst in my conscience. In a flash of shame, I realized just how selfish, uncaring, and hard-hearted I had just been to that young man who needed help. I had brushed him off with the contempt that often comes easily to those of us who have the comfortable necessities of life and then some. "Get out of my way, Jack," this contemptible attitude growls. "I don't care. I don't want to be bothered. Your problem isn't my problem."

What an insensitive, self-centered jerk I was.

I turned the car around and headed back to the gas station, this time hoping and praying that the young man would still be there. And he was. Still standing in the shadows.

I got out of my car and walked toward him, seeing the same despair and embarrassment on his face as before, but also something else. A flicker of fear crossed his eyes as I approached.

This time, I spoke first.

"I'm sorry," I said to him quietly in an unsteady voice clotted with shame. "I'm sorry I didn't help you. It's just that I . . ."

His eyes widened when I took out my wallet and, without looking down to count it, handed him a wad of cash, everything I had, maybe $40.

"I'm really sorry," I stammered again as I turned to walk back to my car, my head down, tears in my eyes.

"Thank you, sir!" he called out to me. "God bless you!"

I've never forgotten that young man. Our chance encounter changed me for the better. Through it, the Lord gave me a searing glimpse of myself in the mirror of truth—the painful truth that though I had always thought of myself as a good and faithful follower of Jesus, I was really, in many ways, when you got right down to it, selfish and apathetic toward the poor and disadvantaged. My arms were loaded full with the good things in life with which God had blessed me—a beautiful wife and family who love me, a comfortable home, plenty of food and drink, a nice car, a good job, some money in the bank—and yet, I couldn't be bothered to share even just a tiny portion of these blessings with someone who had none of those things. And to make matters worse, I very nearly walked away from a huge blessing from the Lord in the person of a beggar who helped me realize my own deep need for conversion.

I thank God with all my heart for that painful moment of grace, for nudging me to turn my car around, go back to that gas station, and help Jesus standing in the shadows. He changed my life.

"He who is kind to the poor lends to the Lord,
*   and he will repay him for his deed"* (Prv 19:17).

"Give to him who begs from you, and do not refuse him
who would borrow from you" (Mt 5:42).

"Then the King will say to those at his right hand, 'Come,
O blessed of my Father, inherit the kingdom prepared for
you from the foundation of the world; for I was hungry
and you gave me food, I was thirsty and you gave me
drink, I was a stranger and you welcomed me, I was
naked and you clothed me, I was sick and you visited me,
I was in prison and you came to me.' Then the righteous
will answer him, 'Lord, when did we see you hungry and
feed you, or thirsty and give you drink? And when did
we see thee a stranger and welcome thee, or naked and
clothe thee? And when did we see you sick or in prison
and visit you?' And the King will answer them, 'Truly, I

say to you, as you did it to one of the least of these my brethren, you did it to me'" (Mt 25:34–40).

"But if anyone has the world's goods and sees his brother in need, yet closes his heart against him, how does God's love abide in him?" (1 Jn 3:17).

Chapter 3

The Waitress

NOT LONG after the youngest of our eleven children was born, my wife and I decided to go out for a quiet meal at a nearby Italian restaurant. We wanted to, you know, have a *quiet* meal.

After showing us to a booth and handing us menus, our waitress started cooing over our infant son, Stephen, asking all the standard questions: "How old?" "Boy or girl?" Etc. Then, she asked the question that neither Nancy nor I particularly wanted to answer: "Is he your *first*?"

It wasn't at all far-fetched for her to ask this, as my lovely wife is slim and young-looking (I'm very proud of how she's kept her figure) and certainly doesn't look like she has eleven children.

Nancy looked at me and, with her eyes, silently said, "Do *you* want to tell her?"

I smiled and shook my head, indicating, "Nah, you go ahead and tell her."

Turning to our waitress, Nancy said breezily, "No, he's our eleventh."

"Wait. What?" the waitress gasped. "You have *eleven children*?!"

"Yes, that's right," Nancy smiled back. "And this is our youngest."

This was too much for our waitress. She scurried off and returned a few moments later with four or five other waitresses who were just as flabbergasted and incredulous as she at this shocking news. It was clear from the expressions on their faces that for a couple to have this many kids freaked them out.

"Why would you have that many kids?" one asked, eyes wide in disbelief. "How do you cope with all that stress?" asked another. As they looked at Nancy, and then at me, and back to Nancy, I could just imagine the pity they felt for her and their indignation toward me. Although none of the waitresses actually said to me, "You monster! How could you keep your wife pregnant all the time like that?" I'm pretty sure a few of them were thinking it.

And then, as if their disapproval wasn't bad enough, the women started detailing their own personal contraceptive habits.

"I'm on the pill," one announced. "We have two kids and that's enough for me!"

"Yeah, well, after our first kid, I got my tubes tied," said another matter-of-factly.

"Not me!" chimed in a third waitress. "Once we got our boy, I made my husband get a *vasectomy!*" They all laughed.

I sat there thinking to myself, *Come on, ladies. I just want to have a plate of lasagna, okay? I really don't want to know all this stuff.*

That's when my wife spoke up. Smiling up at the waitresses, she said calmly, "My husband and I believe that children are a blessing from God. We believe in being open to life so that God can bless our marriage."

That's all she said. But it was enough. Like pouring water on a campfire, my wife's gentle comment was enough to disperse the gawkers at this Big-Family Circus Freak Show. They all went back to work.

An hour later, I paid the check and we gathered up the baby and headed for our mini-van. As we were getting in, I heard footsteps running up behind us. I turned and saw that it was our waitress. In the light of the street lamp above I could see tears glistening in her eyes.

"I'm glad I caught you," she said, slightly out of breath. "I didn't want you to leave before I could say thank you."

(I knew immediately she wasn't talking to me, as I hadn't left that big of a tip.)

She said to my wife, "What you said in there earlier, about how children are a blessing from God. That really stirred my heart. I realized that it's true. You see, my husband and I have two kids, and I'm on the pill. But what you said . . ." she trailed off for a moment, wiping her eyes, "I mean, now, I know that what you said is true, and I've decided I'm getting off the pill. Tonight. When I get off work, I'm going to tell my husband. I don't know how he'll react, but I am going to do it because I want God to bless my marriage. *Thank you* for saying what you said." She gave Nancy a quick hug, turned, and went back into the restaurant. We never saw her again.

I have to think that, someday, at least one person will come up to my wife in Heaven and thank her for speaking the truth about being open to life. "That was my mom you spoke to," he or she will tell her. "Your gentle, providential words changed her life. If it weren't for you, I wouldn't be here."

———————— ··•——◆——•·· ————————

"A gentle response turns away anger" (Prv 15:1, NET).

Speak "the truth in love" (Eph 4:15).

"Now who is there to harm you if you are zealous for what is right? But even if you do suffer for righteousness' sake, you will be blessed. Have no fear of them, nor be troubled, but in your hearts reverence Christ as Lord. Always be prepared to make a defense to anyone who calls you to account for the hope that is in you, yet do it with gentleness and reverence" (1 Pt 3:13–15).

Chapter 4

Biker Guy

THE 500 miles between Columbus, Ohio, and Brevard, North Carolina makes for a pleasant drive through picturesque scenery of rolling hills, lush forests, lakes, and rivers.

What is not pleasant is having car trouble halfway into the trip. That happened to me recently as I chauffeured six teens in our family van to the annual Catholic Apologetics Camp in Brevard conducted by my organization, the Envoy Institute.

The trouble started when we stopped for a bathroom break at an interstate travel plaza in West Virginia and I discovered the van's battery was flat dead. I got it jump-started, and we limped to the nearest repair shop, about five miles away.

The mechanic on duty was a sullen, bald, sunburned, heavily tattooed man in grimy blue coveralls. At about 6' 3" and 300 pounds of muscle, he was the stereotypical Hell's Angel "biker guy."

"My van's battery is dead," I started. "Can you diagnose it for me? I have a bunch of teenagers with me and we need to get down to North Carolina by dinner time."

"Everyone's at lunch," he said flatly without looking up at me. "And I've got other stuff to do right now. Someone'll get to it after lunch, but we've got cars in ahead of yours."

Trying not to let my irritation show, I kept talking in a low-key way, trying to get a little cooperation going. "Hey, I understand. No problem. But any chance you could expedite this for me when your guy gets back from lunch?"

Grudgingly, he put aside whatever he was working on, ambled over to my van, removed the battery, and hooked it up to a diagnostic machine. "This will tell whether you need a new battery or a new alternator."

About fifteen minutes later, he motioned curtly to me to come back to the counter. In a "tough luck, pal, it ain't my problem" tone of voice he said, "Alternator's bad. But we don't sell that kind here."

Of course, I had no way to *get* to wherever they did sell that kind, so I started contemplating my Plan B options and prayed, "Lord! Help me get out of this jam!"

Then, after another twenty minutes of waiting, something amazing happened. Without any change in his gruff demeanor, Biker Guy unexpectedly started showing some actual compassion. First, he got out the Yellow Pages and started calling area auto-parts stores in search of the alternator. Ten minutes later, he had located the type I needed at a shop about ten miles away. Then, he told one of his mechanics to drive me there in his own car, while on his lunch break.

When I got back, though, Biker Guy, explained that because the part wasn't bought at his shop he wasn't allowed to install it for me. "Management," he said with a roll of his eyes and a shrug of his shoulders.

"Tell you what," he said. "I technically can't fix it for you or let you pull the van into the bay, but you *can* use my tools and I'll tell you what to do." That's better than nothing, I figured.

The alternator was located in a very difficult to reach spot. I realized I'd be at this for hours. That's when another amazing thing happened.

Seeing my lack of mechanical skill, Biker Guy said, "*I'll help you.*" He called over another mechanic to help. She was also heavily tattooed, had lots of piercings, a butch haircut, and a cigarette tucked behind one ear.

"*Lesbian,*" I thought to myself sanctimoniously. I'd seen people like these on the news and in movies, or on the street, but never up close. Thanking her for helping, I was surprised by her shy smile and the genuinely kind look on her face. Her compassion didn't at all fit my negative stereotype of a "butch biker chick."

A thunderstorm let loose torrential rain, but they kept working on my van under the open sky, thoroughly drenched and unperturbed by the lightning and crashing thunder. An hour later the new alternator was installed.

When I tried to pay them $60 each (all the cash I had with me), yet another amazing thing happened. They both refused to accept it.

"We all get in tough spots, now and then," Biker Guy said.

Marveling at how their rough exteriors hid hearts of gold, I packed up the teens and drove off, reproaching myself for having secretly judged and looked down on them. I would never have expected those two people to show me the love of Christ. It taught me an important lesson about the danger of my hidden biases.

"*Do not judge by appearances, but judge with right judgment*" (Jn 7:24).

"Love is patient and kind; love is not jealous or boastful; it is not arrogant or rude. Love does not insist on its own way; it is not irritable or resentful; it does not rejoice at wrong, but rejoices in the right. Love bears all things, believes all things, hopes all things, endures all things" (1 Cor 13:4–7).

Chapter 5

Letting Go of Someone I Never Knew

A N ODDLY poignant experience happened to me on Twitter awhile back. Yes, I know, Twitter is hardly the place you'd expect to encounter something poignant, right?

I was pruning and cleaning the list of people I "follow" on Twitter, removing the life coaches, political pundits, self-proclaimed marketing gurus, and those just trying to sell stuff. And in the process of performing this humdrum task, I came to the Twitter profile of Ginger, a Catholic woman whose picture I only vaguely remembered seeing before and whose posts I hadn't seen in quite some time.

Clicking her picture to open the profile, I noticed that her last few posts had been written in the early summer of the previous year and were about her suffering from lung cancer and how her health was deteriorating rapidly. In one post, she spoke of how difficult it was for her to cope with the shock of being informed by her physician that her condition was now *terminal.*

A few posts later, her Twitter feed just . . . ended. There was nothing more.

Fascinated, I googled her name and was sad to learn that she had died later that summer, not long, in fact, after her final post. She was only forty-one and left behind a husband and several children, a few of whom were young.

This melancholy discovery immediately brought to my mind the sad memory of Caroline, a Catholic woman I knew personally and very much admired. She wrote for the magazine I published, and I had worked closely with her for several years. She was a delightful, vibrant, and vital young wife and mom who also died of lung cancer at age forty-four in September of that same year.

Several months before her death, Caroline called to let me know that she had cancer and that it had debilitated her to the point where she could no longer continue writing. She was just too weak and sick. I could hear it in her voice. The lilt in her voice and the happy laughter, which accounted for half of every conversation I ever had with her, was gone. She sounded so tired and didn't laugh—something completely out of character for her. Of course, what was there to laugh about? In that conversation, the last one I ever had with her, she didn't laugh even once.

That's when I realized it was bad, and it hit me that Caroline would be leaving us soon. I tried to push that impossible thought from my mind, hoping and praying, along with countless others who knew and loved her, that she would just . . . get better.

Gazing at Ginger's picture on Twitter, and thinking of Caroline, a pang of sorrow rose up in me. My mouse cursor was poised over the "unfollow" button. I was moved by the realization that, even though she had died some time ago and I would therefore never see any further posts from her, still . . . by pressing "unfollow," I would be, in a certain sense, letting go of her.

It was so strange. After all, unlike Caroline, I had never known Ginger personally but was only aware of her existence through Twitter. And yet, we had a slight connection, albeit nothing more than pixels on a screen.

An image from the movie *Titanic* arose in my mind: the one in which Rose is lying on a piece of floating debris holding on with one hand to the now dead Jack, who is almost entirely submerged in the frigid water. As Rose lets go of his hand, he sinks slowly into oblivion.

I pressed "unfollow," and in so doing said a kind of electronic goodbye to a sister in Christ I never knew, except through the medium of an ephemeral, tenuous, and insignificant collection of pixels on my computer screen. And then, I said a quiet prayer for the repose of her soul.

How strange, and yet, how perfectly fitting, that the Lord would make use of even something as seemingly inconsequential as Twitter to remind the members of his Body of their connection to each other.

Eternal rest grant unto her, O Lord, and let perpetual light shine upon her. May she rest in peace. Amen.

"For as in one body we have many members, and all the members do not have the same function, so we, though many, are one body in Christ, and individually members one of another" (Rom 12:4–5).

"For just as the body is one and has many members, and all the members of the body, though many, are one body, so it is with Christ. . . . The eye cannot say to the hand, 'I have no need of you,' nor again the head to the feet, 'I have no need of you'" (1 Cor 12:12, 21).

Chapter 6

Right Place, Wrong Timing

I ONCE received a letter from a man named Bob, a Southern Baptist in Chicago. He'd heard a radio interview I did and disagreed so strongly with my comments about the Catholic Church that he felt compelled to write and set me straight. He gave a long list of biblical challenges to Catholic teaching on Mary, the pope, the Eucharist, Purgatory, salvation, etc.

Though anti-Catholic, Bob was friendly and respectful. Thus began an interesting correspondence. Months later, when I visited Chicago for a lecture tour of area parishes, Bob invited me to visit his home.

I arrived about 10:00 A.M. and, fortified with endless cups of coffee, Bibles in hand, Bob and I went at it in vigorous discussion for several hours. What began as his steadfast insistence that the Catholic Church was wrong about everything gradually shifted to his being more open to the case for Catholicism. I sensed that the needle on his tolerance meter had gradually moved from the anti-Catholic red zone toward being open to the possibility that Catholic teaching just *might* be true.

Sensing I had to do something bold to push Bob all the way into the convert side of the meter, as I was leaving, I asked if he'd be willing to accompany me to a nearby Catholic parish to see some beautiful life-sized icons. (I had stopped there to make a visit to the Blessed Sacrament that morning.) I figured if I could just get him inside that church, he would be impressed by those icons *and* (my ulterior motive) the grace of Christ in the Blessed Sacrament would bombard his soul and he would *have* to convert to the Catholic Church!

To my surprise, Bob said yes. On the way over, he informed me that, as a Southern Baptist, he had never even been inside a Catholic church before. Baptists, he said, observe the doctrine of separation from non-believers. They generally don't regard Catholics as Christians. He explained that Southern Baptists don't dance, smoke, drink, gamble, or play cards—all activities that they associate with Catholics.

We arrived at the church and, to my frustration, every door was locked! Not to be deterred, we rounded the building and saw a man walking into the double doors of the parish hall, attached to the back of the church.

I knew that, whoever he was, a priest perhaps, he'd let us inside. I was practically giddy with anticipation, knowing that my profoundly effective biblical explanations that day had paved the way for Bob's glorious conversion.

The memory of what happened next remains in my mind's eye like a photograph.

"I hope you like what we're going to see inside, Bob," I said cheerfully, as I opened the door. Neither of us was prepared for what awaited us.

Inside, some 300 people were playing *bingo*. A cloud of cigarette smoke billowed out, washing over us in a fetid wave. As if on cue, a portly man walked past us with four plastic cups of beer pinched in the fingers of each hand. He had *eight* cups of beer and a big smile on his face. There was no telling if he intended to share that alcohol with anyone else.

The room was alive with boisterous gambling, smoking, and drinking Catholics! It was as if I had opened the gates of Hell and said, "Bob, come on in to the Catholic Church!" My Southern Baptist friend's scandalized reaction to this spectacle said everything. We entered the church, looked at the icons briefly, and left. All Bob's prejudices about Catholics had swamped any progress toward conversion that I might have made that day.

To this day, as far as I know, Bob is still a Southern Baptist (no thanks to me). You see, I was (foolishly) trying to convert Bob, assuming that my own efforts of persuasion would be enough to do the trick. How wrong I was! The Bible says, "Speak, Lord, your servant is listening," but in my self-confident vanity I had spent the day doing exactly the opposite. I had been saying, "Listen, Lord, your servant is speaking. When I'm finished here, you can step in and mop up."

Fail.

What I learned that day, I share with you now: I was trying to go it alone. I had lost sight of the fact that only the Lord can convert the human heart. I have trouble enough trying to understand my own heart! What folly to assume that my clever explanations could do the job on their own. Bottom line: I learned to let step back, be patient with God's timing, and to let him do the heavy lifting.

------------------- ◆ -------------------

"Trust in the Lord with all your heart,
and do not rely on your own insight" (Prv 3:5).

"Apart from me you can do nothing" (Jn 15:5).

"Only take care lest this liberty of yours somehow become a stumbling block to the weak. . . . And so by your knowledge this weak man is destroyed, the brother for whom Christ died. Thus, sinning against your brethren and wounding their conscience when it is weak, you sin against Christ. Therefore, if food is a cause of my brother's falling, I will never eat meat, lest I cause my brother to fall" (1 Cor 8:9, 11–12).

Chapter 7

The Pipe in the Pipe

ILAID awake restlessly in bed one evening in 1968. Just eight years old, I was experiencing a strange and upsetting emotion I had never known before, stabbing at me like a small, sharp stick. It was the memory of something bad I had done two years earlier—something I had put out of my mind and for which my parents surely would have (and should have) punished me, had they known. But they had no idea.

No one knew what I did, but *I* knew. My conscience kept me from a deep sleep, like a sharp, little stick jabbing at me with the reminder: "You did that."

What had I done? It was merely a trifle by comparison to the wide array of worse sins often committed after leaving the innocence of childhood.

I was six. Entering my parents' bathroom, I snooped around in search of something, anything, to satisfy my boyish curiosity. I was not supposed to *be* in their bathroom, but since my dad was at work and my mom was busy in the kitchen, I was not deterred.

Turned out, there was nothing interesting in my parents' bathroom, nothing, that is, except for . . . my dad's pipe—the one he smoked in the evenings after work as my mom read and my younger sisters and I played with our toys on the floor. He had told me repeatedly not to touch the pipe.

"Put that down! Those aren't cheap!" he scolded me once when he caught me monkeying around with it. I thought no one was looking. (Parents have a maddeningly preternatural ability to detect mischief.)

But the coast was clear, so I snatched the pipe and proceeded to monkey around with it.

But even a monkey would've been smarter than I because even a monkey wouldn't have panicked and flung his dad's pipe into the toilet when he suddenly heard his mom's footsteps approaching. And not even the dumbest of monkeys would have *flushed the toilet with the pipe in it* as his mom rounded the corner.

It all happened so fast.

Next thing I knew, dinner was over and my dad was in the bathroom plunging the stopped-up toilet. A shout of incredulity and anger emanated from the bathroom.

"What is my *pipe* doing in the *toilet*?!" he bellowed, the plunger dangling limply in one hand as he stared in disbelief at his waterlogged pipe in the other.

Wide-eyed, and knowing I was seconds away from a spanking of Godzilla proportions (my dad's glare had a glint of Godzilla in it), I denied everything, of course. But my lie was not enough. Obviously, *someone* flushed the pipe down the toilet, so I pointed to my younger sister, Lisa, and explained—quite convincingly, apparently—that I saw *her* do it. Lisa, God bless her, was little enough that her denials did not ring true. She received a stern paddling as punishment while I stood by silently, watching her cry.

So there I was years later, tossing and turning in my bed because my conscience was jabbing me with the memory of my three crimes: disobedience to my parents, lying to cover my tracks, and letting an innocent person take the punishment for what I had done.

Shame and remorse forced me out of bed and down the stairs to the living room where my parents were on the couch talking.

It felt like a dam breaking inside me. I just couldn't hold it in and, tearfully, I confessed everything. Convinced I was finally about to get the much-deserved and years-overdue spanking, I was dumbfounded when my folks, pausing and then exchanging a knowing look, told me I was forgiven because I had the courage to tell the truth and face up to what I had done. After a little pep talk about doing the right thing and always being honest, they hugged me and told me they loved me and were proud of me for telling the truth.

Traipsing back upstairs to bed, I was happily surprised and relieved by their loving forgiveness—a reflection of God's love.

I learned a big lesson that night about what happens when one either follows or suppresses his conscience. As an old saying goes:

Sow a thought, reap an act.
Sow an act, reap a habit.
Sow a habit, reap a character.
Sow a character, reap a destiny.

——— •••• ——— ◆ ——— •••• ———

"You shall not bear false witness against your neighbor" (Ex 20:16).

"If we confess our sins, he is faithful and just, and will forgive our sins and cleanse us from all unrighteousness" (1 Jn 2:19).

Chapter 8

The Box of Books

BACK IN 1995, I received an e-mail from a young Catholic law student at Regent University, founded by televangelist Pat Robertson in Virginia Beach, Virginia. "Greg," I'll call him, wrote to say that my book, *Surprised by Truth: 11 Converts Give the Biblical and Historical Reasons for Becoming Catholic*, had helped him fend off a blitzkrieg of challenges from his Evangelical Protestant classmates who, once they discovered he was Catholic, tried their best to convince him to leave the Catholic Church, "get saved," and become a "Bible Christian."

Surprised by Truth is a compendium of first-person conversion testimonies of former Calvinists, Lutherans, Baptists, and others who, as the title suggests, reveal the doctrinal struggles they experienced as they made their way—some, dragged kicking and screaming by God's grace—into the Catholic Church.

I don't know what it was about Greg's e-mail that struck a chord in me. I wrote back asking if he'd do me a favor. "I'd be happy to send you a *case* of those books," I offered, "if you would simply pass them out to your classmates and professors, especially the ones who, you know, have been the most *energetic* in trying to get you to leave the Catholic Church."

"Deal," Greg responded. "I don't know what their reaction will be but, what the heck. I'll be happy to pass them out."

So, the next day, I shipped him a case of forty-four copies of *Surprised by Truth*, saying a little prayer that they'd do some good if placed in the right hands. I can't recall now whether Greg ever wrote me back, but I never forgot his note because it was a nice bit of encouragement and I was happy to know that the book had been a help to him. I could only hope and pray that the box of books I sent him would have a positive effect on those who received them.

Seventeen years after I sent the box, I was signing books at a speaking engagement. A smiling woman walked up to the book table and, pointing toward a stack of *Surprised by Truth* books, said, "That book converted me to the Catholic Church!"

"Really?" I replied. "I'm delighted to hear that. What happened?"

"Well," she said, beaming, "back in the mid-90s, I was in law school at Regent University and one of my classmates, a Catholic, showed up one day with a box of these books. He gave everyone a copy. At first, I was taken aback by the very idea that Evangelical Protestants like me would ever convert to the Catholic Church, but eventually I read it and was powerfully affected by it!"

I never tire of hearing stories like that. And, as it turns out, there was more to that story than I knew. This past summer, during my presentation at Franciscan University of Steubenville's annual Defending the Faith apologetics conference, I recounted this story to the audience. Afterward, a man approached me with information that made my jaw drop.

"I was in that class, too," he told me. "As an Evangelical, I never gave the Catholic Church a second thought . . . until that Catholic student showed up at class with that box of books. I converted to Catholicism and several other students did, too."

"What?!" I exclaimed. "I thought just the one woman had converted."

"No," he smiled. "Besides her and me, I know of at least two others from that class who also converted as a result of reading that book. One of them is now a Catholic priest!"

I marveled at the mysterious power of God's grace. Seventeen years ago, when I impulsively decided to send out that box of books, there was no way I could have guessed how it would change the lives of people I had never met. It felt like I had put a message in a bottle and tossed it into the Pacific Ocean and then, all those years later, found that same bottle washed up on the shore of the Atlantic Ocean.

You never know how your (seemingly random) acts of kindness and generosity can make a great difference for others, even something as simple as handing someone a good book.

———————◆———————

"As he landed he saw a great throng, and he had compassion on them, because they were like sheep without a shepherd; and he began to teach them many things. And when it grew late, his disciples came to him and said, 'This is a lonely place, and the hour is now late; send them away, to go into the country and villages round about and buy themselves something to eat.' But he answered them, 'You give them something to eat.' And they said to him, 'Shall we go and buy two hundred denarii worth of bread, and give it to them to eat?' And he said to them, 'How many loaves have you?

*Go and see.' And when they had found out, they said,
'Five, and two fish.' Then he commanded them all to sit
down by companies upon the green grass. So they sat
down in groups, by hundreds and by fifties. And taking
the five loaves and the two fish he looked up to heaven,
and blessed, and broke the loaves, and gave them to the
disciples to set before the people; and he divided the two
fish among them all. And they all ate and were satisfied.
And they took up twelve baskets full of broken pieces
and of the fish. And those who ate the loaves were five
thousand men"* (Mk 6:34–44).

*"Practice hospitality ungrudgingly to one another. As
each has received a gift, employ it for one another, as
good stewards of God's varied grace"* (1 Pt 4:9–10).

Chapter 9

The VW Bug

FEW THINGS in life are more important to a young man than a car. By the time he reaches eighteen- or nineteen-years-old, having a pretty girlfriend, making money, and finding adventure are at the top of his list of priorities. But he knows, as we all do in this motorized era, that owning a car is an indispensable means to an end if he's serious about pursuing those goals.

Having a car means he's mobile, he's not tied down, he's free to come and go. And if there's anything young men chafe at, it's the feeling of being tethered and unable to make their way in the world and experience life.

That's exactly how I felt when I was a nineteen-year-old college student. I had a pretty girlfriend, a bit of money (burning a hole) in my pocket from my part-time job, and an unlimited appetite for adventure. Living in Southern California made the adventure part particularly alluring, what with the nearby beaches, mountains, Disneyland, and countless other exotic destinations that beckoned. And the beautiful part about the whole thing was that I also had a car, which made having those other things possible.

I say "had" because my jaunty little 1973 Datsun pickup truck (with mag wheels and a four-on-the-floor manual transmission) met a sudden and untimely end when a leaking fuel line sparked an engine fire that completely fried its electrical system. I sold it for scrap. The $300 it fetched me, plus another $200 I scraped together, put me within striking distance of purchasing a cheap replacement vehicle.

I heard that guy I knew was looking to sell his cool-looking 1969 Volkswagen Bug, so I went over and saw that it was in surprisingly good shape. After a few minutes of looking under the hood and a quick test-drive, I offered him $500 for it, knowing that this was a better car (and at a cheaper price!) than any of the jalopies I had looked at thus far.

"Deal," he said. "But I can't let you take it right now because I need it for a few more days, okay?"

"No problem," I told him, disappointed that I couldn't drive off in it then and there. I knew my girlfriend would like riding in this cool car, and I couldn't wait to surprise her with it and take her out for a spin.

A few days later, I was shocked when he told me that another guy I knew named Kevin had offered him $600. "I need the money," he told me sheepishly.

Not so fast, I reminded him. "You promised to sell the car to me! We had a deal! And besides, I really need a car!"

"I need the money," he repeated blandly.

The best I could do was get him to agree to think it over. "I'll bring the money over tomorrow morning if you'll sell it to me. Cash in hand."

"We'll see," he said.

I started praying to God, asking Him to change the seller's mind. "Make him sell me that car, Lord. I *need* a car!" True, but I really didn't need that particular one. After all, there are as many used cars out there as there are fish in the ocean. I fancied a Volkswagen Bug and wanted to cruise around in one with my approving girlfriend. Without realizing it, my vanity was subtly motivating my prayers because I wanted *that* car. "Please, Lord, make him sell it to me."

As I half expected, Kevin got the car (*my* car), and each time I spotted him driving around town, I was reminded that God hadn't answered my prayer.

A month later, Kevin and a friend were killed while driving one night along a twisty road in the hills on their way to a party. As they rounded a particularly sharp corner, one of the Bug's tie rods snapped. It lurched over edge of the road (no guard-rail) and plunged down the slope, becoming a heap of twisted metal and broken glass amidst the trees and boulders at the bottom.

An old adage: *Be careful what you pray for. You may get it.*

Shaken by the realization that I could just as easily have died in a similar wreck, I realized God's no to my prayers for the car was actually a yes to more. He had something much better prepared for me.

I married my pretty girlfriend, and her sporty car became our car. Thirty-five years, eleven children, and eighteen grandchildren later, I'm still thanking the Lord for saying no to me about that car and, in so doing, saying yes to so much more.

"*Call to me and I will answer you, and will tell you great and hidden things which you have not known*" (Jer 33:3).

"*And this is the confidence which we have in him, that if we ask anything according to his will he hears us. And if we know that he hears us in whatever we ask, we know that we have obtained the requests made of him*" (1 Jn 5:14–15).

Chapter 10

Saving Face on Facebook

CHANCES ARE, you have a Facebook account. Having one myself, I'm fascinated at how readily family, friends, and even mere acquaintances and strangers connect with each other there.

This prompted me to write an article called "If You're Married and You're on Facebook, You Should Read This," in which I discuss some of the dangers inherent in exploring other people's Facebook pages, dangers which include: wasting time, unhealthy curiosity about others, and the ever-present temptation to flirt (and worse) online. It's kind of like reading someone's personal e-mail, or their diary, or leafing through their picture albums—and Heaven only knows what that sometimes leads to.

Don't get me wrong. I don't think Facebook is *bad* or that people shouldn't use it, though people who become addicted to it shouldn't. But because Facebook presents a unique set of potential pitfalls, we should exercise a healthy caution when using it.

There are also Facebook *pratfalls* that can befall us. A "pratfall," the dictionary says, is "a humiliating blunder or defeat." They occur more frequently and to more people than you might think, such as when you post an uncareful comment that, to your shock and dismay, attracts angry comments, arguments, and even mockery from others. Perhaps this has happened to you?

In a weird and uncomfortable way, it happened to me, teaching me a life lesson I will never forget.

Someone I knew many years ago—I'll call him John—friended me on Facebook a couple of years ago. I knew his family in the late 1970s and spent a fair amount of time at their house.

John and I had had no contact during those intervening thirty years until he "friended" me and, even then, we didn't actually communicate. He "liked" a few things I posted on Facebook, but that was it. That is, until he sent me a note out of the blue asking me to give a positive online rating and donate money to a secular project he was working on.

I took a look at it but didn't feel I could honestly give it a positive review, much less fork out money to support it. So, I decided to maintain a discreet silence and hope he'd forget he had asked me. No big deal, right? After all, John and I hadn't exchanged as much as a single word for the previous thirty years.

A week went by. Then John sent me scathing message, denouncing me harshly for being "stuck up," "arrogant," and other (worse) things. Was it all because I hadn't responded to his request for money and a review? I was baffled, embarrassed, and irritated.

Trying to save face, I wrote him a conciliatory note, apologizing for whatever it was I could have done to offend him and explaining that, given thirty years of silence, I was perplexed that he would get so angry for no apparent reason. John's response was not at all what I had expected.

His follow-up e-mail was even more ferocious than the first. And that's when I discovered, to my shock and sorrow, what had gone wrong.

John angrily revealed that he had been wounded by something sarcastic I said about him some *thirty-five years earlier*: an offhand joke I made at his expense, the verbal equivalent of tripping someone and laughing at their pratfall. I honestly had no memory of this and probably didn't even give it a second thought the moment I said it. But whatever it was had seriously embarrassed him and, for three decades, John harbored dark anger at me over it. And I was utterly oblivious to it . . . until our bizarre Facebook showdown.

Writing back a sincere apology, I wished him well, and then blocked him. I just didn't see any tidy way to salvage the situation.

I wasn't angry, I was disappointed. Disappointed in myself for having so carelessly and unthinkingly wounded John with my offhand put-down. You know, the kind we all make from time to time. The kind I've made, I'm sorry to say, a million times: a razor-edged witticism at someone's expense that was only intended to be a joke.

Ha. The joke was on me.

I've asked the Lord's forgiveness for my thoughtless stupidity, and His words ring in my ears whenever I'm on Facebook and find myself tempted to post a mean, snarky comment or sarcastic jab at someone.

———————— ••• ◆ •••

"I tell you, on the day of judgment men will render account for every careless word they utter; for by your words you will be justified, and by your words you will be condemned" (Mt 12:36–37).

"If anyone thinks he is religious, and does not bridle his tongue but deceives his heart, this man's religion is vain" (Jas 1:26).

"Do not return evil for evil or reviling for reviling; but on the contrary bless, for to this you have been called, that you may obtain a blessing" (1 Pt 3:9).

Chapter 11

The Bus Ride

I STILL remember exactly where I was and what I was doing the first time someone hassled me for being Catholic. Alright, perhaps *hassle* is too strong of a word to describe what she did, but my memory of what happened remains vivid some forty-five years later.

"She" was Donna—a girl in my fourth-grade class on whom I'd had a secret crush since the first day of school. Graceful, pretty, and doe-eyed with long, dark hair, Donna was friendly and self-confident and much more intriguing to me than any of the other girls in our class. (The character Winnie in the TV series *The Wonder Years* reminds me a great deal of her.)

Little by little, in spite of my gawky shyness, I tried to get her attention. At recess, in the hallways, during lunch, whenever I saw an opportunity, I let Donna know that I liked her. Eventually, she seemed to like me too. Any day after school when I could walk her home and carry her books was pure heaven.

One day, our class piled onto a big yellow school bus for a field-trip to a famous museum. Donna and I sat next to each other on the school bus, gabbing happily all the way there. The outing was great fun. The exhibits were educational and interesting, but by far the highpoint for me was the magical twenty minutes that Donna and I sat together in the darkness of the planetarium show, holding hands.

Life was good! I had arrived. What could possibly go wrong?

Later, as we rode home on the bus, Donna asked demurely, "What church do you go to?"

"Uh, we go to St. Miscellaneous Parish," I said. "What about you?"

Her smile curdled.

"You're . . . *Catholic*?" she asked.

"Yes, I am. Aren't you?" I asked.

"No!"

I paused, perplexed.

"Catholics are idol worshippers," Donna said tersely.

A shadow passed over our conversation.

"We are not!" I retorted, having no clue what an "idol worshipper" was. All I knew was that I didn't want her thinking I was one of them.

"The Bible says we should not carve for ourselves any graven images, and we should not 'bow down to them or serve them' because they are idols, false gods. Catholics bow down to graven images, statues, and that's idol worship!"

"We do not!" I said, though I really had no idea what she was driving at or how I could steer our conversation away from it. My mind was racing. *I* had never worshipped a statue. I had never seen my parents or anyone else worship a statue and, for that matter, I had never even heard of worshipping statues. It sounded so ridiculous.

"But, really, we *don't* worship statues," I pleaded, hoping Donna would take my word for it. She obviously didn't. And, with that, the golden aura surrounding us that day evaporated. Poof. An awkward silence hung between us during the rest of the bus ride home.

Years later, when I began to study my Catholic Faith more deeply, I discovered that the notion that Catholics are "idolaters" is based on a misunderstanding of God's prohibition against worshipping graven images in passages such as Exodus 20:3–6, Numbers 33:52, Deuteronomy 7:5, 2 Kings 17:9–18, and 2 Chronicles 34:1–7. 1 Corinthians 10:14 says, "beloved, shun the worship of idols." But I didn't know this back in the fourth grade.

I also discovered that though God condemns idolatry, he does not forbid religious images per se. In Exodus 25:1, 18–22, He commands Moses to fashion statues of angels to sit atop the Ark of the Covenant! In Numbers 21:8–9, he commands Moses to fashion a bronze serpent and mount it on a pole. Later, when some began worshipping the bronze serpent, the king destroyed it immediately because this once sacred image had become an object of idolatry. Solomon decorated the Temple he built with many statues and graven images of angels, oxen, lions, flowers, and trees (1 Kgs 6:23–35, 7:25, 36), and God blessed him, the Temple, and everything in it (1 Kgs 9:3). Also, Colossians 1:15 declares that Jesus Christ is "the express image" (Greek: *eikonos*, or "icon") of God.

Alas, though, I discovered these biblical truths far too late for them to have been any help to me on the bus ride with Donna that day.

"All scripture is inspired by God and profitable for teaching, for reproof, for correction, and for training in righteousness, that the man of God may be complete, equipped for every good work" (2 Tm 3:16–17).

Chapter 12

Give 'Em Hell

IN THE 1980s, at the height of Madonna's career, one of my sisters became pretty immersed in the ways of the world, trying to emulate the singer's persona and hedonistic values.

I myself had gone through my own worldly phase as a wannabe rock-and-roll star bass player with dreams of becoming the next Paul McCartney. Before the time this story took place I had, by God's grace, experienced a deep conversion in my mid-twenties. Maybe that's why I noticed the spiritual danger right away, while my sister didn't seem to notice. The deeper her fascination with Madonna became, the more concerned I became for her salvation.

Christ declared: "I tell you, . . . unless you repent you will all likewise perish" (Lk 13:5).

Don't get me wrong. I know that, as a sinner, it's hardly my place to be a morality cop. Christ's teaching about the danger of presuming to remove a speck from another's eye while having a log in one's own (*cf.* Mt 7:3–5) was very much on my mind as I worried about my sister. Or, as the old adage goes, "there but for the grace of God go I."

And yet, I knew I had to do something to help her return to the Lord. After all, the Bible also says, "If anyone among you wanders from the truth and someone brings him back, let him know that whoever brings back a sinner from the error of his way will save his soul from death and cover a multitude of sins" (Jas 5:19–20). How could I stand by and say nothing?

Getting her attention was the hard part. How could I effectively deliver the message that she needed to get right with God? My sister knew about my *own* erstwhile struggles with the world, the flesh, and the devil, so I doubted she'd take advice on the spiritual life very seriously if it came from me. That's when it occurred to me that I should let *someone else* give her the advice.

A particular book with a garishly bright red cover—*The Dogma of Hell*, by F.X. Schouppe, S.J.—had deeply impacted my own thinking a few years earlier, reminding me of a truth many people ignore or deny: namely, Hell is real and people really do go there. God does not *send* sinners to Hell as much as they, by rebelling willfully against him and dying unrepentant in that state, send themselves to Hell.

I had an intuition that if my sister would read this book, it could speak to her heart as it had to mine with Christ's teaching:

> "Enter by the narrow gate; for the gate is wide and the way is easy, that leads to destruction, and those who enter by it are many. For the gate is narrow and the way is hard, that leads to life, and those who find it are few." (Mt 7:13–14)

But how do you gracefully give someone a book about *Hell* without giving the impression (which, in this case happened to be true) that you're suggesting she is on her way there? My solution was to give a copy of *The Dogma of Hell* as a Christmas present to my wife and parents and each adult member of my family. (We all were gathered together at my parents' house that year.)

It was a bizarre scene that Christmas morning. So as not to embarrass my sister, I asked everyone to open their present from me at the same time. The looks on their faces were priceless.

I glanced at my sister. With a slight frown on her face, she offered a feeble thank you, but I could tell she was offended. Oh well. The die is cast, I thought. I tried. It's in God's hands now.

About a year later, we had a good laugh and a warm embrace when she told me how that book had indeed changed her heart, turned her around, and helped bring her to conversion. She admitted being mad at first. "I knew the only reason you gave everyone a copy was so I wouldn't realize you meant the book specifically for me." Turns out, though, once she started reading she couldn't put it down. A good sacramental confession followed soon afterward.

You can imagine how happy I was when my sister said, "Thanks for giving me *Hell!*"

--- · ◆ · ---

"The word of the Lord came to me: 'Son of man, speak to your people and say to them, If I bring the sword upon a land, and the people of the land take a man from among them, and make him their watchman, and if he sees the sword coming upon the land and blows the trumpet and warns the people, then if anyone who hears the sound of the trumpet does not take warning, and the sword comes and takes him away, his blood shall be upon his own head. He heard the sound of the trumpet and did not take warning; his blood shall be upon himself. But if he had taken warning, he would have saved his life'" (Ez 33:1–5).

Chapter 13

Miracle Sinus-Headache Cure

I ALWAYS seem to learn life lessons the hard way. They're usually unexpected, and sometimes painful, but each hard-won, new insight helps me become a better person, even though, I'd rather have acquired it with less wear-and-tear on my person.

Case in point: one day, in high school, I discovered a miracle cure for a raging sinus headache I had *and* learned in a roundabout way the truth of Romans 8:28: "We know that in everything God works for good with those who love him."

You see, I played soccer in high school. I also wore glasses; actually, I've worn them since I was five. Sometime during soccer season that year, my aviator-style glasses (I know. Hideous, right? But cut me some slack, please. We're talking 1977 styles, after all) suffered a minor malfunction when one of the nose pads was snapped off. That left a nose pad on the right side of my nose and a little metal spike on the other side.

At that time, my parents didn't have much money, so a new pair of glasses weren't in the family budget, especially since I could keep wearing them for a while, even if their lopsidedness made me look even more like a complete dork. I was also lazy when it came to speaking up about something as insignificant as a missing nose pad on my glasses.

So, I just wore them as they were: slightly tilted up on the side with the pad, and tilted down slightly on the side that just had a little metal spike resting on the left side of the bridge of my nose. It wasn't comfortable, but it wasn't painful either, and so I just went with it. As you can imagine, and not just because of the goofy glasses I wore, I was not what you could call a babe magnet at that particular time. (Nor am I suggesting that I am one now, for that matter.)

At that same time—maybe you can see where this is headed—I also developed a bad head-cold that progressed into a severe sinus headache. You know, the kind of wretched headache caused by the sinus vapor-lock that makes it feel like your eardrums are going to explode? That's the extremely uncomfortable situation I was in because my head was so pressurized. No amount of yawning would open my ears even the tiniest bit to allow some of the built-up pressure to equalize. I still remember how painful that unrelenting headache was.

For the life of me, though, I don't remember why I didn't just ask my parents to take me to the doctor and get some relief! My guess is that it was simple inertia. I could function well enough to get through the day, so I just put up with my hyperbaric-chamber head, waiting for it to subside as this problem had done before. I was one miserable cowboy that week.

So, one afternoon during soccer practice, I was on the bench (where I spent most of my time, as it happens) talking with a teammate next to me when, POW! one of the players kicked the ball out of bounds and straight into my face, knocking me backward off the bench, my glasses flying from my head.

I lay there stunned and embarrassed. My dorky aviator glasses had snapped in two, though not before rendering me one final, signal service.

Rather than get mad or embarrassed, I was happy! A big smile of relief wreathed my face. Why? Well, that little metal spike where the nose pad had snapped off had neatly punctured my nose cartilage just high enough to tap into my sinus and—*whoo boy!*—all that pent up pressure came out in one very satisfying, audible pop. I was so relieved at how instantaneously the pain had left me, that I've never forgotten it to this day.

I don't mean to suggest that *God* arranged things such that I'd get hit in the face by that errant soccer ball. That was just a dumb accident. But what stuck with me is how a problem was solved in a completely unexpected way. You know, the way God sometimes answers our prayers, not with the answer we were expecting or hoping for. Sometimes, he answers prayers in very unexpected ways that, even so, help us overcome some problem.

Oh, and yes, when I went home after soccer practice that day and smilingly showed my mom and dad the broken glasses, they did shell out for a new pair. Regrettably, though, I selected another pair of aviators.

———————— ••• ——◆—— ••• ————————

"We know that in everything God works for good with those who love him, who are called according to his purpose" (Rom 8:28).

"In this you rejoice, though now for a little while you may have to suffer various trials, so that the genuineness of your faith, more precious than gold which *though perishable is tested by fire, may redound to praise and glory and honor at the revelation of Jesus Christ"* (1 Pt 1:6–7).

"So we do not lose heart. Though our outer nature is wasting away, our inner nature is being renewed every day. For this slight momentary affliction is preparing for us an eternal weight of glory beyond all comparison, because we look not to the things that are seen but to the things that are unseen; for the things that are seen are transient, but the things that are unseen are eternal" (2 Cor 4:16–18).

Chapter 14

St. Joseph to the Rescue

YEARS AGO, my wife and I tried—in vain, for two frustrating years—to sell our house. Nothing worked. We had priced it competitively; it was a modest though very presentable home, and it had "curb appeal," as real-estate agents like to say. We figured it would sell quickly, but as each month rolled by with hardly a showing, much less an actual offer, we began to despair of ever finding a buyer. What made things even more baffling was that other homes similar to ours were selling just fine all around us.

Despondent and discouraged, we were about to give up when one of my wife's friends, a well-meaning fellow Catholic from our parish, excitedly suggested that we buy a little plastic statue of St. Joseph and . . . bury it upside down in our yard. "Doing that will guarantee your house sells quickly!" she insisted breathlessly. "Other people have tried this technique, and it worked for them. Some bury him in the front yard, some in the back yard, some upside down! But it seems to really work. You should do it too!"

Nancy and I glanced at each other and rolled our eyes at this advice but politely thanked the lady and told her we'd keep it in mind. But when her friend was out of earshot, we both agreed that it was a silly idea.

As far as I was concerned this bury-St.-Joseph thing was just an urban legend, and it couldn't be true even though everyone seemed to swear they knew someone who had sold a house that way. Kind of like the "flash your headlights and die" urban legend—i.e., that gang members, looking to initiate a newbie by making him kill someone to prove his loyalty, would cruise around after dark with their lights off just waiting for someone to flash his lights as a courtesy warning that they were off. The unlucky person who flashed his lights first would be targeted and killed for kicks. A lot of folks believed this was real, but it was as fake as the Easter Bunny.

Another couple of months went by without even a nibble on our house. Nancy and I were starting to get desperate.

"Honey," she said sheepishly one evening at the dinner table, "maybe . . . we ought to think about . . . burying the St. Joseph statue. After all, what do we have to lose? We've tried everything and just can't sell the house."

"No," I shook my head. "We can't do that, although, I admit it's tempting. But it's really just a popular superstition. You know, like believing that rubbing a rabbit's foot will bring you good luck, or that walking under a ladder or breaking a mirror will give you *bad* luck. A lot of people swear by these things, but they just aren't true."

"Well, our friend says it really works. I know it's silly, but, like I said, what have we got to lose by trying it?"

"How about this?" I countered. "I know we both agree that it's just superstition—even if, here and there, some people may have actually gotten lucky and sold their house after burying a statue of St. Joseph in their yard. It just doesn't sit well with me because it gives the impression that we can *force* St. Joseph to spring into action and do our bidding just because his statue is buried upside down. But if you really want to give it a shot, just for fun, you can do it. But just don't *tell* me you did it so that I'll have some plausible deniability."

We both laughed at how silly the whole thing sounded and agreed that we wouldn't take the superstition route to sell our home.

A few weeks later, Nancy had a great suggestion: "Why don't we start a novena to St. Joseph?! As Catholics, we know that prayer is the most powerful thing we can do."

"Excellent point, honey," I smiled. "And the Bible says that 'the prayer of a righteous person is very powerful in its effects' (Jas 5:16). Aside from Our Lady, I can't imagine that there's a saint in heaven more righteous than St. Joseph." So, we started the novena.

Nine days later, on March 19th, *the feast of St. Joseph*, our realtor called to say that, out of the blue, she had received an offer on the house for the price we were asking. We were stunned. The buyer put down a deposit that same day and we had the house under contract by dinner time.

Thank you, St. Joseph! I think you were trying to tell us something.

———— •·•—————◆————— •·• ————

"*Have nothing to do with godless and silly myths. Train yourself in godliness*" (1 Tm 4:7).

"*Formerly, when you did not know God, you were in bondage to beings that by nature are no gods; but now that you have come to know God, or rather to be known by God, how can you turn back again to the weak and beggarly elemental spirits, whose slaves you want to be once more?*" (Gal 4:8–10).

Chapter 15

The Plane Ride

THIS EARTHLY life is filled with countless mundane, routine, and often trivial tasks and yet, when we have "ears to hear and eyes to see" (Mt 13:16, NLT), these otherwise commonplace duties can yield up important intuitions and insights that float into view when we don't expect them. That's how it's always been for me (at least when I'm paying attention). The Lord invariably teaches me life lessons through the outwardly insignificant and humdrum activities of my everyday life.

For example, I recently gained a helpful insight while travelling to Phoenix for a speaking engagement. Columbus, Ohio, where I live, was damp and chilly the morning of my departure. The skies were gray and overcast, and I was really looking forward to escaping the dreary bleakness of those leaden skies into the sunny, wild-blue yonder of the Arizona desert.

So, I'm seated on the plane, getting ready to take off. I prefer an aisle seat, but this morning I find myself seated next to the window, where I have a nice view of the dismal clouds. We take off, and the plane quickly climbs through the clouds toward what I hope will be a comfortable cruising altitude, where my mind will be free to move about the universe.

Gazing absentmindedly out the window, I watch the clouds fall away beneath me as we ascend. The plane glides upward through the lowest cloud layer, and we enter a clear and significantly brighter gap between cloud decks. It's bright enough for me to see a fair distance away, although there's really nothing to see except more clouds. I take in this view for a few minutes before the sky begins to darken and become obscured as the plane rises through another layer of clouds.

Nothing but gray for the next few minutes, and rather bumpy, as passing through clouds typically causes turbulence. Nothing unusual there. We're rising higher, and still, all I can see is a wall of gray, formless clouds.

Suddenly, we slip into another clear zone. This time, though, I can see for miles and miles. It's far brighter up here, though I still can't see the azure blue sky I've been expecting. Craning my neck to look upward, I see yet another layer of clouds above us, this one lighter and thinner than those below. A few minutes later, we plunge upward into those clouds, suffused with light and hints of blue peeking through, here and there.

That's when it occurs to me how similar this flight is to the spiritual life. This simple metaphor stirs my soul with thoughts about my own personal journey toward Heaven. I know that "somewhere up there" is the clear blue sky—Heaven—where I want to be. Where I belong. Where God created me to be happy with him forever.

There's nothing I want more than to someday, when my appointed time here on earth has concluded, escape the gray, dreary clouds, the mist, and the turbulence of this imperfect earthly life and enter into the warm, tranquil light above in the heavenly life to come. To get there, though, I am reminded that I must pass through who knows how many more cloud layers that may loom above me, between where I am now and where I am headed.

The great spiritual masters, such as St. Augustine, St. Francis, St. Teresa of Avila, St. John of the Cross, St. Catherine of Siena, St. Francis de Sales, and St. Therese of Lisieux, all tell us the same thing: our upward path to Heaven leads through the various stages of purgation and illumination before it finally arrives at the blessed union of love with God for which we were made and to which he ceaselessly beckons us.

Like you, I've passed through any number of dark and difficult clouds in my life and, like you, I know well life's turbulence, ambiguity, and unpredictability. Many a time I've thought to myself, "Hey! I've made it!" only to realize with a sigh, "No. More clouds ahead. I still have a good way yet to go."

One day, though, sooner or later, those who love God will pass irrevocably beyond the interminable clouds of this earthly life and find themselves enveloped within the splendorous light and glory of Heaven, which is marvelously and infinitely better than anything even Arizona can offer.

----------◆----------

"I consider that the sufferings of this present time are not worth comparing with the glory that is to be revealed to us" (Rom 8:18).

"For now we see in a mirror dimly, but then face to face. Now I know in part; then I shall understand fully, even as I have been fully understood" (1 Cor 13:12).

"Beloved, do not be surprised at the fiery ordeal which comes upon you to prove you, as though something strange were happening to you. But rejoice in so far as you share Christ's sufferings, that you may also rejoice and be glad when his glory is revealed" (1 Pt 4:12-13).

Chapter 16

Caroline

A FRIEND and colleague of mine died of lung cancer on September 11, 2009, and I still find myself thinking about her, missing her, and trying to make sense of why God would call from this life such a wonderful, creative, loving, and joyful woman and take her so early from her husband and young children. Her name was Caroline. She was just forty-four when she died, never having smoked a cigarette in her life.

I see her in my mind's eye as she always seemed to be: mirthful, smiling, and gabbing away enthusiastically about something new and interesting that had turned up along the way in her full, busy life as wife and mother. She was the vibrant center of many concentric circles of family, friends, and parish life. Caroline's ready laughter was contagious and her cheerful optimism a tonic for those around her. She always seemed to find the lighter side or the silver lining in a difficult situation.

I cannot imagine the anguish Caroline's husband, children, and family experienced when she died. I only worked with her. They lived with her. Their pain was surely beyond words. For my part, in the weeks and months after she passed, I felt an ache of sadness each time something chanced to remind me of her and that . . . she was gone.

Losing Caroline was a double loss for me in that she would no longer contribute to *Envoy Magazine*, a Catholic journal I published for many years. A gifted writer, she contributed clever and interesting articles and also wrote a regular column for us. As we collaborated on the magazine, it was clear to me that each issue was better for her presence in it.

We took a hiatus from printing *Envoy*, due to a lack funds, but when the financial picture greened up again, Caroline was the first person I called to see if she could resuming writing for us. I was delighted when she said yes. Neither of us knew, however, that she had only a year left.

Months later, one cold November evening, Caroline called to let me know that she had cancer and that it had debilitated her so rapidly (because it had been detected so late in its course) that she was too weak to continue writing.

I could hear the deep exhaustion in her flat, weak voice. There were no bubbles left in her normally effervescent repartee. Her laughter, which liberally punctuated every conversation I'd ever had with her, was simply gone. Of course, what was there to laugh about?

Caroline's wheezy, shallow breathing told me she was in bad shape, though I didn't realize just how bad. What strength she had left, she told me, had completely collapsed, and her ability to focus her thoughts and write had drained away.

That phone call was the last time we ever spoke. I kept telling myself I'd get around to visiting her but never did. My life was too busy, I told myself. And besides, I'd see her next week, or the week after that for sure. She wasn't dying that quickly, after all, right? But one week stretched into another until, one day, there was no more time left. Every last grain of sand had passed through the center of the hourglass of her life, from time into eternity.

When Caroline died, my sadness was tinged with bitter regret for having so foolishly delayed visiting her until it was too late. The upside was that I learned a valuable, though painful, lesson. I'll never procrastinate like this again, I told myself, not when someone is ill and in danger of dying. But that belated resolution did nothing to make me feel any better about having dragged my feet. This will just be another sore regret I'll have to carry around for the rest of my life, I thought. But Caroline had the last word on this.

Two years later, I was at EWTN to film a television program. At lunch, I sat next to a woman who was also at the studio to record an interview about her apostolate of helping terminally ill pilgrims who visit the Marian shrine at Lourdes in hopes of a cure.

"Oh, I've wanted to meet you," she said with a sparkling smile, "ever since I assisted an American wife and mother named Caroline who came to Lourdes. She told me you were her good friend and said several times how much she enjoyed working with you for *Envoy Magazine*."

My eyes widened in wonder and gratitude to God as she related how, at Lourdes, Caroline had spoken to her about me. Of all people. That balm of grace changed everything for me. I still feel a bittersweet twinge whenever I remember my failure. But, by God's grace, it has been, ever since, far more sweet than bitter. Thank you, Lord. Thank you, Caroline.

Here is a sample of Caroline's gracious, grace-filled writing:

It Doesn't Get Any Better Than This!

By Caroline Schermerhorn

As I write this column, I am tucked away in an elegant two-room suite at a northern Michigan golf resort. It is a cloudy, but temperate, fifty outside. Between the lovely gas fireplace in our suite, and an inviting hot tub in the bathroom, some romance and relaxation are a sure bet this weekend.

Having never swung a golf club, I don't have the usual kind of appreciation for the legendary Weiskopf "Legend" course outside the sliding glass doors. However, there is something exceptionally beautiful about having breakfast while overlooking the eighteenth hole.

We got here last night after a pleasant eight-hour drive, just my husband and I. No Barney tapes, no extra potty stops. I didn't even have to share my drink. We grooved to classic rock, drove for hours without stopping, and guzzled one $2.00 iced cappuccino after another. The car was uncommonly clean, the back seat empty except for our suitcases and a hanging bag with an elegant party dress, suit, and tie. We drank in our old camaraderie, telling jokes, sharing stories, or just holding hands and thinking to the familiar beat of the windshield wipers.

I was in seventh heaven.

"This is the life," I thought.

When we arrived at the resort, we were seated to a candlelit dinner, tucked away in the dim corner of an elegant restaurant. A talented pianist tinkled the ivories of a shiny black grand piano.

". . . and what will you have, young lady?" I looked into the decidedly young eyes of a well-dressed waiter. Young lady? I felt like royalty.

No dishes, no crises. I didn't even have to get up from dinner to find the second ketchup bottle deep in the recesses of the refrigerator. Could anything be so luxurious? "This is the life," I breathed, sipping a before-dinner drink from a fine crystal glass.

This morning, my husband has a couple of meetings to attend, so I'm alone until lunch time. Completely, gloriously, and unapologetically alone. I sink into the sofa, pour myself a soda, choose an old black and white movie, and settle in for an after breakfast cat nap. With no other person "home" at the moment, I have no needs to look after—except my own. A bubble bath? A quiet bike ride?

This is the life!

We stay up late and sleep in later all weekend long.

By Sunday, I feel just about as relaxed as I've ever been. The smell of morning inspires me to sketch and write as I relax.

Our ride home is equally delightful. We thoroughly enjoy that easy-going, conversational, uninterrupted mode of sharing that we had when we first met.

Once home, it's time to pick up the children from the various friends who took them in for the weekend. One stop at a time, the six children and their luggage crowd the van, which has been so empty since Friday.

Happy to see each other, hugs and kisses go all around. Almost instantly, the calendar is out, and we are trying to figure out the following day's schedule. Little League practice was moved up a day, and play rehearsal occurs in the same inning. Dinner needs to be made, bath times scheduled, and laundry cleaned.

Our solitude is a memory of yesterday. The time alone, focused on the eyes of my beloved, is just another twinkle to reminisce over.

Later, in the twilight of the evening, I smell the clean blond curls of my youngest. I savor the sounds of laughing and screaming from the trampoline. I immerse myself in the thoughts voiced by my lovely teenage daughters.

Bedtime hastens. One at a time, I feel the sweet closeness of six goodnight hugs. The eldest disappears up the stairs. The day is over, and I'm ready for bed, too.

But wait, there is one more to attend to . . . the six-year-old has slipped back downstairs for "one more hug." His breath is warm on my ear as he whispers, "Mommy, I missed you."

This is the life.

"Do not boast about tomorrow,
for you do not know what a day may bring forth"
(Prv 27:1).

"We must work the works of him who sent me, while it is day; night comes, when no one can work" (Jn 9:4).

Chapter 17

A Narrow Escape

SOME YEARS ago, while on a trip to Rome, my friend Dave and I were out late one evening doing a bit of sightseeing around St. Peter's. From there, we started walking back toward our hotel about two miles away. When we reached the summit of a steep hill, we decided to stop at a restaurant for a nightcap. At about midnight we paid our bill and headed out into the night to walk the rest of the way. (When in Rome, I've learned, walking everywhere is the best way to stay ahead of all the wonderful food.) A little further on, needing a bathroom break, we ducked into a McDonalds. That's when our otherwise pleasant evening quickly began to go bad.

"Something's not right," Dave said, furrowing his brow as he glanced at the dozen or so patrons clustered at their tables and at the counter placing orders. "I just saw a guy in here who was also in the restaurant where we stopped for a glass of wine. What are the odds he would show up here, too?"

"That can't be a coincidence," I agreed. On edge, we exited McDonalds, intending to walk that last mile to our hotel as rapidly as possible. No such luck.

Crossing quickly to the other side of the street, we glanced back and saw several men burst outside and spread out, clearly looking for us. "That's him!" Dave said under his breath. Realizing we were in more jeopardy out on the dark street, we scuttled back toward the well-lit McDonalds. I darted inside just as several thugs gathered threateningly in a semi-circle around Dave, who was on the sidewalk, his back to the wall. This was bad. These guys clearly intended to do something unpleasant to us, robbery perhaps not being the worst of it.

Now we were panicked. Two of us against, what, six or eight of them? No way could we possibly beat those odds. Getting robbed and beaten up looked likely. I had to think fast. Exiting the McDonalds through its side door, I rounded the corner where Dave was trapped and shouted "Hey, everybody! How's it going?!" This distracted them just enough for Dave and me to bolt back inside. The gang of guys joined us too, eyeing us menacingly and murmuring to each other in Italian what I assumed were the details of their nefarious plan.

There seemed to be no way out of this dangerous predicament. Our hotel was over a mile away down a dark street. We were on foot, and there was no one we could call for help. Worse yet, McDonalds would be closing soon and we'd be back out on the street, precisely where our assailants wanted us.

"We've got to pray, Dave," I whispered. "We're in real trouble." Afraid and out of options, I silently prayed a Hail Mary and an Our Father and—I am not exaggerating—within about one minute, a Catholic priest I recognized walked in and up to the counter to order. Nonplussed, I sidled over and addressed him in Spanish, hoping the thugs wouldn't understand.

"We're in a dangerous situation here, Father," I said, "and we really need your help." I explained what was happening. He nodded and, in Spanish, told me that his priest friend was waiting in the car just outside at the curb and they would drive us back to the hotel. Relieved but still worried we'd get jumped I signaled to Dave to follow the priest. He got his bag of food, turned and walked out, with Dave and I right behind him.

"It's okay!" he told the other priest as we darted outside and piled quickly into the car locking the doors. The gang, befuddled by this unexpected development, followed us out but not quickly enough to do anything except watch in frustration as we drove off unscathed.

What did I learn from this? Two things. First, it's not wise to be out and about, on foot, late at night in a foreign city. Not even the Eternal City. Second, no matter how difficult and hopeless the situation, we should pray for the Lord's guidance and protection. So often, it seems to me, I don't get it because I don't ask for it. The power of prayer became very real and very meaningful to me that night.

* * *

"Though I walk in the midst of trouble,
*   you preserve my life;*
you stretch out your hand against the wrath of my
*   enemies,*
*   and your right hand delivers me"* (Ps 138:7).

Chapter 18

The Death Cookie

I CONSIDER the summer between my junior and senior years of high school my "Golden Summer." Living in Southern California (Orange County) was a great place to enjoy summer fun, given the wide variety of entertainment and attractions within easy driving distance: Disneyland, Knott's Berry Farm, the beach, the mountains, etc. It was also a big plus that I had recently gotten my driver's license and was able to come and go pretty freely, as long as my parent's second car, a station wagon, was available.

But what made that summer especially golden was Christie, a pretty, blonde, Protestant girl I had started dating. We went out for pizza, saw movies, went roller skating and swimming, and generally had a great time hanging out together as much as possible that summer. It was fun!

What was *not* so fun, however, was the price I had to pay Christie's dad for being allowed to go out with his daughter. Her dad, a pleasant and sincere man, was an ardent born-again, Bible-believing Protestant, who, I soon discovered, did not regard Catholics to be true Christians.

"The Roman Catholic Church," he informed me early on, "is a counterfeit religion. It teaches a false gospel and worships a different Jesus than the Jesus of the Bible." Turned out, his negative attitude toward the Catholic Church did not translate into a negative attitude toward me personally, which was great because I'm sure he would have run me off immediately if he hadn't liked me. So, at least I had that going for me.

The price I paid for being allowed to date Christie? Whenever I would come over, her dad made sure that he and I spent some "quality time" in a "biblical" conversation— sometimes one-on-one in their living room, sometimes with Christie and her mom sitting with us—meaning that he'd sit there with his well-worn King James Bible open on his lap and interrogate me (always with a smile on his face!) about stuff like how well I knew Jesus, how I could get saved, how the Bible is the sole rule of faith for Christians, and how all those distinctively Catholic teachings I had been raised to believe were, you know, doctrines of demons from the pit of Hell. (Yes, Christie's dad actually said those words).

Being far more biblically knowledgeable than I, he challenged my Catholic beliefs relentlessly, trying to get me to leave the "darkness of Romanism" and get born again. I was pretty much defenseless. I knew *what* I believed but his challenges made me painfully aware that I really didn't know *why* I believed it. But rather than fold, I decided to dig in and do my homework to find the answers to each new objection he raised against Catholicism.

My parents—God bless them—had a large library of Catholic books in our home, including classic works of apologetics from the early part of the twentieth century, such as the excellent three-volume *Radio Replies*. To my happy surprise, these books contained superb biblical and historical answers to every single anti-Catholic argument Christie's dad had been pummeling me with.

As the summer wore on, I was gaining confidence in my beliefs because I was discovering that no matter how plausible his case against the Church was, the Catholic response made far more sense to me biblically and historically and, for that matter, logically. And so, as time wore on, his efforts to drag me out of the Catholic Church had the unintended effect of making me a stronger, more knowledgeable, and more confident Catholic.

One day in August, while Christie and I were hanging out by her pool, her dad came out with his Bible to "chat" with me. The subject this time was the Catholic doctrine of the Real Presence of Christ in the Eucharist. He handed me a Fundamentalist comic-book tract called *The Death Cookie*.

"Read this, Pat," he said. "It explains why the Romanist doctrine of worshipping a cookie is not biblical but of the devil."

By now, this kind of thing didn't bother me much. I stuffed the tract in my pocket, promising to read it, which I did, later that evening. It was laughable. The *Death Cookie*'s pseudo-historical and biblically contorted arguments against the Eucharist were so outlandish, so ridiculous and easily debunked that I found myself wondering if Christie's dad had ever really known what the Catholic Church actually taught on this subject or if he was just going on what he'd heard about Catholicism. It sure seemed to me that he was attacking something he didn't really understand.

The day he handed me *The Death Cookie* was, as I look back on it now, the day I began to feel truly confident and secure in my Catholic beliefs because that's when it really started to dawn on me that all the anti-Catholic arguments Christie's Dad had thrown at me during that "Golden Summer" had already been effectively and decisively refuted by Catholics long before me. With books like *Radio Replies*, I found myself sitting on the shoulders of giants, as the saying goes. All the work of answering these challenges had been done long ago, and I found myself the grateful recipient of that priceless information.

Not long after I read *The Death Cookie*, things with Christie began to fizzle. Maybe it was because she (and, more particularly, her dad) realized I wasn't going to leave the Catholic Church. Or maybe it was because my newfound confidence made conversations with her dad less pleasant and, therefore, my visits to their home less tolerable. I don't know.

I do know, though, that all the "Death Cookie" arguments against the Catholic Church I grappled with that summer had exactly the opposite effect on me than the one Christie's dad had intended. And for that I will be eternally grateful to him.

"First of all you must understand this, that no prophecy of scripture is a matter of one's own interpretation, because no prophecy ever came by the impulse of man, but men moved by the Holy Spirit spoke from God" (2 Pt 1:20–21).

"And count the forbearance of our Lord as salvation. So also our beloved brother Paul wrote to you according to the wisdom given him, speaking of this as he does in all his letters. There are some things in them hard to understand, which the ignorant and unstable twist to their own destruction, as they do the other scriptures" (2 Pt 3:15–16).

"Beloved, do not believe every spirit, but test the spirits to see whether they are of God; for many false prophets have gone out into the world" (1 Jn 4:1).

Chapter 19

Suffer the Little Children

IN MATTHEW 19:14, the Lord says to his meddlesome disciples, "Suffer the little children, and forbid them not to come to me: for the kingdom of heaven is for such."

This verse came to mind one day as I read a blogpost written by a twenty-something Catholic blogger named Amy, the mother of two. It seems Amy was trying to say a few prayers after morning Mass but couldn't concentrate due to a spat she overheard in the vestibule between a sixty-something woman and another young mom. Turns out the older lady was rebuking the younger lady because of the noisy distraction her kids had caused during Mass.

The young mom, God bless her, stuck up for herself and her buckaroos, and Amy, who walked over, found herself drawn into the squabble, siding with the Young Mom. I believe I would have done the same, had I been there.

Yes, I can relate to Young Mom, doing her heroic best to participate at Mass with her rambunctious kids in tow. But I also sympathize Older Woman's exasperation over the commotion during Mass. As often happens, this hot-button issue raised tempers, making it difficult for these three women to remain charitable and understanding toward each other.

As the father of a large family myself (eleven kids), I know from experience how, at times, kids can be awfully irritating to those around them during Mass with their noise and fidgeting and such. Most of my children are now adults, several with their own children, and they just reinforce my sympathy for young families who are learning (hopefully, they are learning) how to control and shush their children when they need to at Mass.

A few times, when we were young parents, Nancy and I got some cranky remarks and pinch-mouthed scowls from older parishioners who were irked because our kids made noise during Mass. My attitude then was, "Hey, kids are kids. Noise happens. Comes with the territory. Get used to it."

But in truth, I must admit that, as I've grown older and wiser, I also have a great deal of sympathy for the cranky scowl-mouths who are irked by noisy kids at Mass. Yes, they, like all of us, should strive to be patient and forbearing toward those noisy families who, whether through negligence or simply being overwhelmed, do not do enough to keep the kiddos in line.

There's room for improvement on both sides of the divide. I know this personally because, now that I'm a grandfather of eighteen with more than a little gray hair, I sometimes catch my inner cranky scowl-mouth coming out when obstreperous kids at Mass start to get my goat.

At our excellent parish, there are plenty of families who have lots of kids. I'm talking counter-cultural-to-the-third-power lots of kids. Most of these fine and devout Catholic parents are adept at the art of swiftly rising from the pew and hustling a talkative, crying, screaming, or otherwise disruptive child out of Mass and into a hallway.

This is good and pleasing in my sight.

But some parents, not many, don't seem to have learned a lesson of basic courtesy that I believe should be included at some point in a couple's marriage prep classes, and, that is,

"Thou Shalt Not Irritate Everyone in the Church to the Point of Distraction by Allowing Your Disruptive Child(ren) to Remain in the Pew and Make Everyone Else Miserable Simply Because YOU WILL NOT DO THE RIGHT THING AND GET UP AND TAKE THE CHILD OUT OF CHURCH *BEFORE PEOPLE'S HEADS START EXPLODING.*"

Ahem.

Those parents must understand that by allowing their child(ren) to make loud noise during Mass is an injustice to everyone else, and it is very bad form. It's inconsiderate at best. Maybe the lector should add one additional announcement before each Mass starts, right after the reminder to turn off your cell phone: "Parents, if your children get fussy and noisy during Mass, please, out of charity to those around you, take your children outside until they settle down."

I think that's perfectly reasonable, don't you? As I see it, if this modest request were routinely made in Catholic parishes, while never neglecting to welcome, embrace, encourage, and support large and rambunctious Catholic families (like mine)—they are an important part of the future of the Church, after all—there'd be one less reason for anyone to get irritated, the parents of fidgety kids wouldn't feel put upon, and nice ladies like Amy would be able to pray their post-Mass thanksgiving prayers in peace without being drawn into squabbles like the one she described.

——————————— ••• ——◆—— ••• ———————————

"Have nothing to do with stupid, senseless controversies; you know that they breed quarrels. And the Lord's servant must not be quarrelsome but kindly to everyone, an apt teacher, forbearing, correcting his opponents with gentleness" (2 Tm 2:23–25).

Chapter 20

The Cheesecake

MY FIRST real job was as a fry cook at the cafeteria in a local department store. On my sixteenth birthday, a really nice girl, who worked in the housewares department, surprised me with a deluxe birthday gift at the end of our shift.

"I heard you like cheesecake," she smiled, handing me a large, pink bakery box. "So I thought you'd enjoy this. Happy birthday!"

Oh, baby, I thought to myself, my mouth watering as I raised the lid expectantly. I was not disappointed. Inside was a magnificent, freshly made, deep-dish cheesecake topped with a massive pile of fat, succulent blueberries. She was right. I did love cheesecake, and this one she had purchased so thoughtfully for me at a local bakery looked insanely good. I couldn't wait to get home and have me some—it being my birthday and all. I thanked the girl profusely (flattered that she would go out of her way to do something so nice for me).

Proudly bearing my extravagant birthday gift before me the way I imagined the Wise Men might have carried their gold, frankincense, and myrrh to Baby Jesus, I sauntered out to the parking lot where my dad was waiting to drive me home. He seemed impressed. He had an "I'm-gonna-have-me-some-of-that" look on his face when I lifted the box top to give him a peek.

When we got home, my mom, dad, and I sat down at the kitchen table and enjoyed a slice of the delicious cheesecake. What we ate accounted for maybe twenty-five percent of the whole thing. I went to bed feeling very self-satisfied. My best birthday present yet, as far as I was concerned.

About 2:00 in the morning, I awoke with a persistent thought beating like a drum in my mind: my cheesecake is down in the kitchen waiting for me. I lay there weighing my options. On the one hand, it was 2:00 in the morning and everyone in the house was fast asleep. I should stay in bed. But on the other hand, hey, my cheesecake was down there in the kitchen waiting for me. And, I reminded myself, it was my cheesecake, after all. My teenage sense of autonomy asserted itself violently in that moment, demanding that I stride downstairs and take for myself what was rightly mine—all 17 billion calories of it.

And so I did.

Tiptoeing down to the kitchen, I removed the pink box from the fridge, sat myself at the kitchen table, and—I kid you not—devoured the entire thing. And to make an already dire situation exponentially worse, I blithely washed it all down with a tumbler of ice-cold Hawaiian Fruit Punch. (There is a great deal one does not understand about life and the digestive system at age sixteen.)

Oh baby! "Life is good!" I thought as I traipsed back upstairs to my bed, supremely pleased with myself for having boldly asserted my rights over my birthday gift. How could anyone fault me? I remember thinking to myself as I drifted off into a content, cheesecake-ridden slumber.

A few hours later, I awoke with a start. Something bad, something really, really bad, was happening in my abdomen, the part of me where I had foolishly deposited all that cheesecake and Hawaiian Fruit Punch. Saying I was *sick to my stomach* does not adequately describe the sensation of doom that assailed me in that moment.

And for the entire next day, I was violently ill, alternately retching and resting, as I tried to expel from my body (in all ways known to man) every last molecule of the cheesecake that tormented me so.

My parents, upon learning the specifics about how I came to be in this predicament, didn't get angry with me, but they did point out that I had to live with the consequences of my very bad decision to polish off the rest of the cheesecake all by myself.

I have lived with the results of that cheesecake fiasco. Not only did I develop an inflexible and enduring dislike for cheesecake, I also learned from my sin of gluttony a very important lesson about the virtue of moderation (temperance). Even though, technically, that cheesecake belonged to me, I was a fool to think I could power down the whole thing without any negative side effects. In other words, too much of a good thing can be bad for you. And, believe me, eating the rest of the cheesecake was very bad for my frame of mind, not to mention the health and well-being of my stomach.

In the end, though, I learned an important truth from this unpleasant experience: just because I can do something doesn't mean I should.

"'All things are lawful,' but not all things are help-ful. 'All things are lawful,' but not all things build up" (1 Cor 10:23).

"If you have found honey, eat only enough for you,
    lest you be sated with it and vomit it" (Prv 25:16).

Chapter 21

The Angry Wife

SOME YEARS ago, a Protestant fellow I'll call Tom called my office one day and asked if I'd answer some questions he had about the Catholic Church. It was the first of several long phone conversations about the Faith we'd have over the next several weeks.

Tom explained that, as a Southern Baptist who grew up in a small Midwestern town, he'd had few opportunities to encounter faithful Catholics and even fewer to get to know the Catholic Church on its own terms. Instead, he had marinated for several decades in the strongly anti-Catholic attitudes of his family, friends, and other members of the fundamental Bible church he attended.

"No problem," I said. "There are a lot of common questions people ask about the Church, and I'll do my best to give you good answers. It's not that complicated, really."

"No, really," Tom insisted. "I don't just have *questions* about the Catholic Church, I'm questioning everything I've ever been told about it! Practically everyone I know and love thinks the Catholic Church is of the devil. Seriously. I was raised to believe that the Catholic Church is a counterfeit form of Christianity—corrupt and full of man-made traditions—and that Catholics honor God with their lips but their hearts are far from him."

Over the course of our long phone conversation, Tom related how, until just recently, he had been convinced that Catholics worshiped "another Jesus" and followed a "different [i.e., false] gospel" (2 Cor 11:4), believing they can earn their salvation by doing a lifetime of good works. But his curiosity about the Catholic Church had been piqued, seemingly out of the blue, by a chance conversation with a Catholic he met on a business trip.

At first, Tom said, he "kind of hassled" the Catholic guy with several standard arguments he had learned to use with "Romanists." But he was surprised and disarmed by the fact that his interlocutor wasn't rattled, didn't get angry or defensive, and actually had some reasonable answers. Before they parted company, the Catholic guy wrote down my website on the back of his business card and suggested Tom contact me. Apparently, that conversation really got his wheels turning in a big way.

After discussing several of his biblical questions—Mary, the pope, salvation, purgatory, etc.—I offered to send Tom some books and audio recordings to help him study these issues in greater detail.

"That would be good," Tom said, but explained earnestly, "I have to be really careful how I go about investigating the Catholic Church because my wife, Kathy—a Baptist preacher's daughter—is adamantly convinced that Catholics are lost. When I told her that I was just *curious* about knowing more, she pretty much blew up at me."

When Kathy realized that Tom's was more than just a passing curiosity about things Catholic, she laid down the law then and there, informing him that if he *ever* even *thought* about becoming Catholic, she'd divorce him and take their three kids with her. She was that alarmed and angry that he would even consider that path.

"That's why, whatever you do, Patrick, it's crucial that we keep our conversations about the Catholic Church absolutely confidential. And whatever materials you send me, please be sure to send them in a plain, unmarked package because, if my wife finds it, I really think she'll make good on her promise to divorce me." I assured Tom I'd use the utmost discretion.

I packed up a small box of books, including my own *Surprised by Truth* and a couple of CDs, all of which delved into aspects of the Catholic Church he and I had been discussing. I said a little prayer for Tom as I dropped the box off at the UPS shipping station, hoping the materials would be helpful to him in his journey.

God's providence is a funny thing, as is proven by what happened next. Even though Tom worked from home, and even though Tom was expecting the package and was planning to take the delivery out in the driveway before his wife knew about it, the UPS truck happened to arrive early that day, about ten minutes *after* he had darted out of the house to run a quick errand.

Tom's wife answered the door and signed for the package, a plain, non-descript brown box addressed to her husband. Her curiosity lit like a match and, as she closed the front door behind her, she shook the box trying to discern its mysterious contents. She opened the box and, to her horror, discovered a passel of *Catholic* books and CDs, and she instantly understood what it meant.

Tom got back home ten minutes later to find Kathy had locked herself in their bedroom and wouldn't come out. "I can't believe you're actually going through with your insane interest in Roman Catholicism!" she shouted angrily at Tom through the locked door. "It's a *false religion!* I'm not going to be married to a *Catholic!* I'm leaving you and taking the kids."

Tom was completely distraught by this horrifying turn of events and, locked out of his own bedroom, spent the night on the couch miserable about the looming breakup with his wife and torn between his love for her and his growing attraction to the Catholic Church.

Early the next morning, Kathy woke him, kneeling next to the couch. Groggy and disoriented by sleep he asked her what was wrong. "Are you okay? Is one of the kids sick?"

"No," she answered, wiping tears from her eyes. "Nothing's wrong. I'm sorry about what I said last night. I've been thinking about it, and if you want to explore the Catholic Church I won't fight you. I'm sorry. I understand now what you're going through.

Incredulous, Tom rubbed his eyes and asked Kathy what on earth had happened to cause this change in her.

"Well," she said, with a hint of a smile, "When I opened that box I became furious at you because I realized you were secretly thinking about becoming Catholic. So I locked myself in our room. But then I realized *I locked myself in the room with that box*. And after a while I got bored. So I started reading the book. I've been reading all night and couldn't sleep because of everything I discovered. I understand a little better now, and I won't oppose you."

The happy ending? Yes, Tom did convert and come into the Catholic Church not long after that. And so did Kathy. And so did their children. Proof that God does indeed work in mysterious (and seemingly coincidental) ways.

"For my thoughts are not your thoughts, neither are your ways my ways, says the LORD" (Is 55:8).

Chapter 22

Short-Changed on the Foreign Exchange

NEAR THE end of my junior year, I entered a school-wide competition at my high school designed to choose a foreign exchange student for the next year. I was one of at least fifty other students who applied, so I didn't think I had a great shot at winning, but given my long-time fascination with Japan—its people, language, culture, and history—I decided to try anyway because becoming a foreign exchange student was the only way I figured I'd ever have a chance to visit Japan, immerse myself in its culture, and, truth be told, meet some pretty Japanese girls.

"What the heck!" I thought. "You can't win if you don't play, right?" My parents agreed to let me apply and duly signed all the permission slips. I was in. One of the questions on the application was, in order of preference, what three countries would I most like to visit if I were chosen to go? I wrote down: Japan, Japan, Japan.

I prayed fervently every day that God would grant my heart's desire to win the competition. My teachers thought I had a good chance, my parents had given their permission, and of course it was something I really wanted and knew would be good for me in many ways.

As the selection process narrowed, I became more excited and hopeful each time I made the cut. From the initial fifty applicants, the committee picked twenty semi-finalists (myself included) to continue. We had to jump through a variety of hoops, including one-on-one and group interviews and writing an essay on why we wanted to be foreign exchange students. There were group activities, contests, and outings designed especially (I discovered later) so the committee could observe how we interacted with one another and learn what kind of people we were. Introvert? Extrovert? Sore loser? Team player? Diva? Generous? Loner? Class clown? Plays well with others? Makes friends easily? Etc.

The committee kept notes about each of us (I discovered later) and compared them in closed-door meetings. The field of twenty semi-finalists then narrowed to five finalists: three girls and two guys. To my happy astonishment, I made the cut.

Another round of interviews followed, as well as one final event—a backyard pool-party barbecue—so the committee could give us a final once-over before making their decision.

When the committee chairman called to tell me that I had been chosen and that I would be spending my senior year in Japan, I was delirious with elation and immediately began making plans and telling everyone the great news. *"I'm going to Japan!"*

Several weeks later, though, my elation collapsed into ruins when the committee chairman called my parents to inquire whether it was true that we would be moving to a new town outside the school district during my senior year. (Apparently, I had mentioned this detail inadvertently along the way.)

My dad confirmed that, yes, he and my mom were planning to move that fall. "Well," the response came, "we expect the exchange student to come back to school and share his experiences with everyone, and if you're living outside the school district, that would be pretty difficult."

No amount of my pleading did any good. I promised I'd do anything—crawl over broken glass, if need be—to come back to the high school and share my foreign exchange experiences. It didn't matter. Because of the impending move, I wouldn't be going to Japan after all. The runner up would go in my place.

Darkness descended. Even now, nearly forty years later, I remember how angry, disappointed, and depressed I was then. Why did my parents have to move?! Why did God close the door on my dream?! It was a tough several weeks for me, made all the worse when my school threw a bon voyage party for the guy who took my place. I didn't attend.

Only later, though, did it dawn on me that God had, in fact, answered my prayers and in a vastly more wonderful way than I had expected. "No, you are not going to Japan, at least not yet," he was saying, though I couldn't hear it through the cocoon of disappointment that had enveloped me.

If I *had* gone to Japan then, I never would have met Nancy, the beautiful young woman I fell in love with and married and with whom God has blessed me with eleven great sons and daughters. Our eighteen grandchildren wouldn't be here. And all the countless other blessings that God has bestowed on Nancy and me along the way in our thirty-five years of marriage would never have happened. Oh, and it turns out I have visited Japan many times, too, which is icing on the cake.

The lesson for me is clear: sometimes God doesn't say yes to our prayers for things we want because he wants to give us something far, far better.

"Many, Lord my God,
are the wonders you have done,
the things you planned for us" (Ps 40:5, NIV).

Chapter 23

The Lost Girl

Afterward being out of town for several days doing back-to-back speaking events, I arrive home tired. Needing sleep, I lay down on my bed for a nap. Next thing I know, my wife is shaking me awake, saying something urgently about our five-year-old daughter Rebecca.

"What?" I ask, blearily. "What's going on?"

"We can't find Rebecca," Nancy says in a tone reserved for statements like, "The house is on fire."

"Rebecca? What?!" I leap up, instantly wide awake. "What do you mean she's *missing*? I saw her just before lying down. She's got to be here somewhere."

"We've looked everywhere," Nancy insists. "We've ransacked the house and looked everywhere outside, in trees, everywhere, and Rebecca's not here. The last time I saw her, she was outside playing in the yard."

The terror I see in Nancy's eyes arcs like an electric current into me, and I frantically begin searching the house. "We've already looked for her!" Nancy says again, "she's vanished. She's not here! And I waited till I had searched everywhere before waking you."

My worst nightmare as a parent—one of my children being abducted—was unfolding in hideous, nightmarish detail as I pick up the phone and call 911, giving them a description of our daughter, a strawberry blonde, blue-eyed, freckle-faced pixie.

Uttering the words, "My five-year-old daughter is missing, and I think she may have been taken," is beyond surreal. This kind of thing only happens to other people, not to me, runs through my mind again and again.

Within five minutes the first of several police squad cars pulls up in our driveway. If our daughter has been abducted, the officer informs me grimly, every second counts in trying to find her. They scour our home and yard and soon confirm our worst fear: our little girl was gone. My mind fills with jet-black dread as the unthinkable crashes down on me in a wave of horrifying reality: my daughter has been abducted.

Soon, a sheriff's helicopter is circling above our neighborhood scanning the yards, roads, fields, and woods around our house. Sheriff's deputies go door-to-door in our neighborhood showing Rebecca's picture asking for any information anyone might have.

"Mr. Madrid," an officer informs me, "we're going to need a statement from you." We walk over to his cruiser and I sit in the passenger seat trying to hold it together as the officer asks me where I was and what I had been doing for the past several hours. If my daughter has been abducted, my world is over. Life as I've known it is over, and a life-time of misery and aching emptiness is just beginning.

Minutes later, another officer strides over to the cruiser and raps excitedly on the window. He's grinning. Then Nancy rushes out onto the driveway, smiling widely and screaming with joy: "They *found* her! They *found* her! She's *okay!*"

I feel like a popped balloon. All the emotional pressure building up inside vanishes instantly as I hear the glorious good news that my little girl is safe, unharmed, and on her way home.

Nancy and I embrace. There are tears of joy and relief, laughter, and more tears.

So what had happened? Well, Rebecca, being a curious little sprite, had decided to explore our eldest daughter's car. A portion of the back seat pulls down to allow access to the trunk. She climbed through the hatch and, once inside the trunk, the hatch snapped shut, locking her in. Ten to fifteen minutes later, our older daughter got in her car, turned up the stereo, and drove to work, never hearing Rebecca knocking from inside the trunk, trying to get her attention.

About an hour after she got to work, Bridget got a frantic call from my wife telling her to come home because Rebecca had gone missing. Explaining the emergency to her boss, Bridget grabbed her purse and rushed out to her car only to find two policemen and an anxious looking woman standing there.

"Is this your car, miss?" one of the officers asked with a look of suspicion.

"Yes," Bridget stammered, "but why? What's wrong?"

"We need you to open the trunk of your car, miss. Right now."

Stunned, Bridget opened the trunk and, to everyone's amazement, little Rebecca was curled up inside, blinking at the bright light, and though cold and scared, no worse for wear.

Turns out, the woman had pulled her car into the spot next to Bridget's and, improbably, happened to glance into the backseat area and noticed a spare windshield wiper blade being poked repeatedly out through the back seat from the trunk. She realized someone was trapped *in* the trunk and called the cops.

Once Rebecca explained to the police how she managed to get trapped inside, the pieces of the puzzle fell into place and Bridget brought her home to us straight away. The joy and relief Nancy and I experienced was overwhelming. This happened eleven years ago. Rebecca is sixteen now and the star of her high school varsity soccer team. One thing about my life *did* change forever that day, and for that I'm very grateful. I realized just how suddenly and drastically life can change and, therefore, that I should never take anything or anyone for granted. Each day, each person is a gift.

"O give thanks to the LORD, *for he is good;*
for his mercy endures for ever! (Ps 107:1).

Chapter 24

The Roller Coaster

A MUSEMENT PARKS are supposed to be, you know, amusing. Which is why, when something happened to me at one that was anything *but* amusing, it made a lasting impression. Years ago, Nancy and I invited Brian and Kim and their kids (we've been close family friends for many years) to join us and our kids at a major theme park for a day of carefree fun in the sun. We lucked out that day with flawless summer weather: a cloudless, beautiful blue sky, low humidity, and temps in the high seventies—ideal for enjoying the rides and strolling leisurely through the park till the sun went down and it was time for a hearty dinner and a swim in the hotel pool.

Like most young people, in my youth I was quite keen on roller coasters and took every opportunity to get my thrill on whenever I had a chance to take a ride on one. The faster, taller, and scarier the better as far as I was concerned. But as I grew older (and wiser), my need for speed diminished. This is pretty common. Which is why, when we entered the amusement park that morning, our older kids all darted off in a pack straight away for the roller coasters, while we parents hung back and ambled along with our strollers and young kiddos.

Later in the day, though, our teens prevailed on Brian and me to go up with them on the park's tallest, fastest wooden roller coaster (one of the tallest, fastest, and longest wooden roller coasters at that time). What could possibly go wrong?

It'll be a *blast*, they said. You'll *love* it, they said. It'll be *just like when you were young!* they said. And so, with that appeal to my long-lost youth ringing in my middle-aged ears, I decided, what the heck! and accompanied them to the ride.

Settling into the car with my grinning nine-year-old son sitting next to me, we dutifully strapped in with our seat belts, and then the heavy-metal padded bar swung down automatically against our chests, ensuring that, come what may, we wouldn't be thrown from the car in the event of an unexpected and highly-unlikely problem. *Cool!* My boy and I exclaimed to each other as the ride glided forward, slowly at first.

At first, the *cha-chink, cha-chink, cha-chink* of the roller coaster's steady upward climb along the wooden track was familiar and reassuring as we headed toward the pinnacle. Giggling and glancing at each other with excitement, my son and I held our breaths as we neared the summit just before the first long drop.

Then, just before we crested the top, everything stopped. The cars froze at what felt like a forty-five degree angle, leaving us staring straight up into that azure, blue sky, hundreds of feet in the air (it felt like thousands), the heavy metal bars holding us firmly in place as we waited for . . . something to happen.

Five minutes passed, and nothing happened. There was no movement and no clue of what might be happening. All I knew was that I was motionless in sky, looking up into the wild blue yonder while to my right and left, all I could see was a *very* long drop down to the asphalt where—somewhere— my wife was waiting for me.

And that's when it hit me. At first, it was just a mild, slightly nagging, nervous feeling. *I don't like this.* But within a minute or two, my dark discomfort had expanded into an *I'm seriously unhappy here* burst of panic.

What could possibly go wrong? As I hung there in the sky with my little boy who, as yet, had not registered any apprehension with our problem, I figured that there must be some insignificant technical problem the ground crew would soon resolve, and we'd be on our way. In the meantime, I did my best to cheer up my son (and myself) and distract him (and myself) from the fact that we were stuck—on a thin ribbon of steel on a rickety wooden track—in the sky, with an endless drop below down to *terra firma*. And there we sat, face up and motionless on a wooden scaffolding to oblivion.

Five minutes had passed. Then ten minutes. By twenty minutes of being stranded, my imagination began to take over. I had been through the desert on a horse with no name, and I started to panic. My chief fear was that somehow, no matter how improbable, the wooden roller coaster my son and I were trapped inside of (the heavy metal bar locking us in place, after all), somehow *the thing would catch on fire and we would be trapped.*

Yes, I know, it was an absurd and irrational notion that this wooden ride could catch on fire, but I confess that this fear suddenly gripped me in its vice-like grip for what seemed an eternity, which in reality was no more than another fifteen minutes. That the ride *could* catch on fire was beyond reasonable, and yet, my fearful imagination latched onto this wild improbability with a choke-hold that surprised me. Before long, park personnel had clambered way up the narrow catwalk alongside the track and helped us all exit our cars, seemingly a thousand feet in the air, and make our way safely down the spidery steps back toward the safety of *terra firma*.

In the end, all was well. But I learned something unexpected and unsettling about myself: how quickly I had succumbed to my own "what if?" paranoid worries about something as implausible as the wooden roller coaster catching on fire. My lesson? To put into practice Jesus's words.

"Consider the ravens: they neither sow nor reap, they have neither storehouse nor barn, and yet God feeds them. Of how much more value are you than the birds! And which of you by being anxious can add a cubit to his span of life? If then you are not able to do as small a thing as that, why are you anxious about the rest? Consider the lilies, how they grow; they neither toil nor spin; yet I tell you, even Solomon in all his glory was not arrayed like one of these. But if God so clothes the grass which is alive in the field today and tomorrow is thrown into the oven, how much more will he clothe you, O men of little faith!" (Lk 12:24–28).

"We know that in everything God works for good with those who love him, who are called according to his purpose" (Rom 8:28).

"Be strong and of good courage; be not frightened, neither be dismayed; for the Lord your God is with you wherever you go" (Jos 1:9).

Chapter 25

Teach Your Children Well

WHEN I was a small child, my mom and dad both worked full-time jobs to make ends meet. This meant that they had to put me in day-care which, in the early 1960s, was pretty uncommon compared to how prevalent it is nowadays.

My mom landed a job in the medical records department of a large Los Angeles-area Catholic hospital that happened to offer day-care for the children of its employees. It was staffed by several Carmelite nuns from Spain who, as it happened, did not speak any English. This meant that for eight hours a day, five days a week I was immersed in Castilian Spanish at just the right age to learn it quickly and easily.

Although my dad is 100% Hispanic (Spanish and Mexican), and my paternal grandparents, aunts, and uncles all spoke Spanish like in "the Old Country," we only spoke English at the home. I think this was because, in those days, it was quite common for immigrants to the United States to eschew their native languages in favor of better assimilation into mainstream American culture. Consequently, their first-generation children often wound up never learning their parents' native language. Not so in my case.

When I was about five-years-old, my dad's work situation had improved enough that my mom was able to stop working and return to being a stay-at-home housewife ,(which was great for my younger sisters and me because, hey, it's *great* to come home from school every day with mom waiting for us, sometimes with a cold glass of milk and a plate of freshly baked chocolate chip cookies). Anyway, I gradually forgot all about that stretch of time I spent in the Spanish-only day care.

When I got into high school, something unexpected and fortuitous happened. My Spanish 101 class was weird for me because, for some reason I couldn't fathom, it seemed that I already knew a lot of Spanish vocabulary words and basic grammar.

"How do you *know* this information, Patrick?" I recall my first-year Spanish teacher asking me incredulously one day after I had aced a test with ease. I honestly didn't know what to tell her. Truth be told, I wasn't what you might call a very motivated student in those days, and I knew that my inexplicable proficiency in Spanish had little to do with my study skills, such as they were. I continued to excel at Spanish and became quite an avid *conversador* (conversationalist). I figured I just had a knack for languages.

One day, though, my mom solved the mystery when she informed me that I had learned a great deal of Spanish when I was very young. I hazily remembered the nuns but not that they had spoken only Spanish to us. That's when I realized that it wasn't that I had a particularly robust skill at learning foreign languages, it was just that I had a great deal of it already stored on my mental hard-drive from back when I was little.

Years later, as I was raising my own children, I reflected on this dimension of my life and realized how apt a parallel it is to teaching children the Catholic Faith. Just as it's practically effortless for kids to learn another language when they're young, it's just as effortless for them to acquire the basics of the Faith when they're young. Which means, parents, grandparents, Godparents, if you make a sincere and persistent effort to teach children at least the basics of the Catholic Faith—and much more than the basics, to the extent you're able to—they will not only assimilate them easily and quickly, they will, most importantly, *retain* those truths as they grow into adulthood, especially when they move into those treacherous waters that flow through adolescence and young adulthood.

The Bible says in Proverbs 22:6, "Train up a child in the way he should go, and when he is old he will not depart from it."

Becoming fluent in Spanish was a great boon to me and it opened many doors and other opportunities to me in my professional career that would have remained closed otherwise. I'm grateful for the life-long gift those Spanish nuns gave me by immersing me in that important language when I was the perfect age to learn and retain it. But that gift, as great as it was, cannot compare with the immeasurably greater gift my parents gave me by raising me firmly in the Catholic Faith from my earliest days. May God reward them!

In my case, I was able to navigate the rough waters I passed through in my younger years as a result of the solid training in my Catholic Faith I received from my parents, parish priests, teachers, and others who helped enkindle in me a flame of love for God and a desire to pursue holiness that, yes, often flickered when worldly winds of temptation and distraction swirled around me.

Whether you teach your children in English, Spanish, or any other language, make every effort to teach them the truth, "God loves you and he wants you to love him back!"

In due time, they'll spend eternity praising God and thanking you.

"Train up a child in the way he should go,
  and when he is old he will not depart from it"
(Prv 22:6).

"Jesus said, 'Let the children come to me, and do not hinder them; for to such belongs the kingdom of heaven'" (Mt 19:14).

"Do your best to present yourself to God as one approved, a workman who has no need to be ashamed, rightly handling the word of truth" (2 Tm 2:15).

Chapter 26

Gate B-32

PUBLIC SPEAKING has been a major part of my professional work for nearly thirty years now. This involves crisscrossing the United States, which means passing through countless airports along the way. One particular week, at the conclusion of a speaking tour at multiple parishes within the Archdiocese of Boston, I arrived at Boston Logan Airport for my flight home. The weather in Boston that day was raw, rainy, and dreary. That may have been why, as I waited a few hours in the American Airlines terminal for my (weather-delayed) flight, my mind turned to somber things.

I began pondering the fact that, at 7:45 a.m. on September 11, 2001, American Airlines Flight 11 pulled back from the gate at this very airport and commenced its journey into death. I deduced that whichever gate it had departed from must be somewhere near where I was seated.

I realized that, though I had flown in and out of Boston Logan Airport many times over the years, I had never stopped to think of its historical importance as one of the starting points of the terror attacks on the United States that terrible, beautiful, cloudless morning. The doomed United Flight 175 also departed from Boston Logan that fateful day, pulling back from Gate C-19 at 7:58 am, its unsuspecting crew and passengers having but one more hour to live.

I rose and made my way toward a cluster of idle T.S.A. workers standing near the security checkpoint to ask which gate Flight 11 had departed from on 9/11.

"B-32," they all said flatly and without hesitating, pointing out the window to an American flag atop a departure ramp way down at the far end of American Airlines terminal, fluttering and snapping in the stiff, rainy wind. Thanking them, I walked down the terminal, passing through throngs of passengers and airport workers toward an important historical monument that nobody else seemed conscious of.

Surely, many others in the airport knew the significance of Gate B-32, right? American Airlines gate agents, pilots, flight attendants, T.S.A. folks must all know it. But as I strode toward the end of the terminal, I had the eerie feeling that maybe I was the only person at that moment who was preoccupied with the grim memory of what happened in that place on September 11. I realized that Gate B-32 will forever be to Boston what the Sixth Floor is to Dallas, what Ford's Theater is to Washington, D.C.

As I walked, I imagined myself there that morning, approaching Gate B-32, seeing the five murderers arrive as well, their minds writhing with hatred for America and Americans. A line from "Riders on the Storm," The Doors' anthem of doom, flashed into my mind as I tried to envision the hijackers going about their deadly errand:

> There's a killer on the road
> His brain is squirmin' like a toad
> Take a long holiday
> Let your children play

If ya give this man a ride
Sweet memory will die
Killer on the road, yeah

When I got to Gate B-32, I was both surprised and not surprised by how completely ordinary it was. Passengers were coming and going, a gate agent stood behind the counter typing on the computer. It could have been any other nondescript gate at any other nondescript airport anywhere.

In the years since 9/11, countless passengers and flight crews have passed through that very doorway and through that very jet-bridge on which the killers and their innocent victims walked that historic morning. Do they feel anything different? Do they realize where they are? No. They don't. Gate B-32 is an exceedingly significant historical place, but nobody seems to realize it.

There is no commemorative plaque or sign to signify what happened there, just the understandable, real-world obliviousness of all those anonymous passengers, endlessly arriving from and departing to points unknown, getting on with their lives.

Just that and a forlorn yet defiant American flag snapping in the wind and rain.

Post Script: I have been a loyal frequent flyer with American Airlines since 1988, logging over 3 million miles with them. Sometimes, as I settle into my seat for a flight, I wonder if I might ever have flown in the particular 767 aircraft which was Flight 11 on 9/11. The chances are fair that at least once I did. Was I ever aboard a flight served by any of the pilots or flight attendants who perished on Flight 11? It's possible. I hope so. Thinking about that makes them more real to me. I've prayed for them and their passengers many times ever since they walked for the very last time across the threshold of Gate B-32.

------------------◆------------------

"Let your loins be girded and your lamps burning, and be like men who are waiting for their master to come home from the marriage feast, so that they may open to him at once when he comes and knocks. Blessed are those servants whom the master finds awake when he comes; truly, I say to you, he will put on his apron and have them sit at table, and he will come and serve them. If he comes in the second watch, or in the third, and finds them so, blessed are those servants! But know this, that if the householder had known at what hour the thief was coming, he would have been awake and would not have left his house to be broken into. You also must be ready; for the Son of man is coming at an hour you do not expect" (Lk 12:35–40).

Remember those "who through faith conquered king-doms, enforced justice, received promises, stopped the mouths of lions, quenched raging fire, escaped the edge of the sword, won strength out of weakness, became mighty in war, put foreign armies to flight. Women received their dead by resurrection. Some were tortured, refusing to accept release, that they might rise again to a better life. Others suffered mocking and scourging, and even chains and imprisonment. They were stoned, they were sawn in two, they were killed with the sword; they went about in skins of sheep and goats, destitute, afflicted, ill-treated—of whom the world was not worthy—wan-dering over deserts and mountains, and in dens and caves of the earth. And all these, though well attested by their faith, did not receive what was promised, since God had foreseen something better for us, that apart from us they should not be made perfect" (Heb 11:33–40).

Chapter 27

The Mosque

A S PART of my work in apologetics (i.e., giving a
reasoned defense of the Faith), I started studying Islam
in the early 1990s so I could improve my ability to share my
faith in Jesus with Muslims and answer their questions and
objections about Christianity.

For about six months I read several books on the subject,
as well as a good deal of the Qur'an, and I listened to several
lectures on cassette tape by a South African Muslim apologist
named Ahmed Deedat. A lively and flamboyant preacher, his
single goal in these lectures was to discredit Christianity and
its beliefs, especially the Trinity and the divinity of Jesus. I
learned a great deal from these resources but realized I needed
to go deeper if I wanted to acquire sufficient command of the
issues involved in Christian-Muslim dialogue, so I decided
to visit a mosque and learn more from real live Muslims.

The mosque I visited was down the street from a major
university, so I figured I'd find a variety of Muslims, not just
Americans. To my surprise, though I did notice a couple of
Westerners, almost everyone was Middle Eastern. An Arab
man in his early thirties greeted me in good though strongly
accented English as I strode through the main door.

"Hello, my name is Ahmed. How may I help you?"

"Hi, I'm Patrick," I responded smiling. "*As-salam alaykum*" (one of the few Arabic phrases, meaning "peace be upon you," that I had memorized in preparation for my first visit to a mosque). I expected the customary response, *wa alaikum salaam,* but he simply nodded to me, not quite smiling, and again said, "Hello." (I discovered later that some devout Muslims, due to religious scruples, do not exchange this Arabic greeting with non-Muslims).

"I've never been to a Mosque before," I said. "I'm Catholic, and I would like to know more about Islam. I have a lot of questions." At this, Ahmed smiled, his guarded manner a little less guarded. "Very good! We would be happy to answer them." I explained that though I was a convinced Christian I was still fascinated with Islam and wanted to understand the religion better. All of this was true, of course, but the bit I didn't mention was that I also wanted to learn how to more effectively explain and defend the divinity of Jesus Christ with Muslims.

My first visit to the mosque lasted about an hour. Ahmed gave me a tour of the place. In addition to the mosque itself, there were several large meeting rooms, a kitchen and dining hall, a wing of classrooms, and a special room adjacent to the restrooms for ritual washing of hands and feet before entering the prayer area. Ahmed invited me in to observe afternoon prayers, which were due to start in a few minutes.

It was a large open room with a few tall, narrow windows, the floor covered with ornate rugs. It was devoid of any furniture except for a single chair set inside a small niche in the middle of the far wall. "That is where the imam sits during Friday prayers," Ahmed explained. I sat quietly in the back, praying my own prayers as a Catholic. Perhaps fifty men (I saw no women there that day) knelt to pray, all facing the wall with the niche (facing the city of Mecca), bowing their heads to the ground repeatedly.

Afterward, Ahmed and I spoke for another twenty minutes or so before I left. I made an appointment to return the following week.

The next time I came back, Ahmed introduced me to half a dozen Muslim men all in their twenties and thirties. They asked me a few mildly challenging questions about Christianity, though some seemed genuinely curious. All of them were university students, hailing from Egypt, Kuwait, Iraq, Syria, and (including Ahmed) Saudi Arabia. They all spoke English reasonably well but with heavy Arabic accents. And they were all eager to explain the basics of Islam to me, Ahmed taking the lead in our discussions, which usually were held in one of the meeting rooms. The mood was friendly and relaxed, and I asked every possible question about Islam I could think of, some of them intended to round out what I had read in the books and heard on the tapes I studied ahead of time.

At the end of my third visit, they asked me to come back the following week and have dinner with them. To my surprise, we ate a magnificent meal of lamb, rice, vegetables, and Middle Eastern bread sitting on the floor. The food was served communal-style on large platters, though there were no utensils. Everyone ate with their hands. I inquired about this and Ahmed explained that because Mohammed was known to dine seated on the floor using no utensils, it was customary to imitate his practice.

After dinner and an intense but friendly conversation about Islam and Christianity, we watched a videotaped debate between a Protestant minister and . . . guess who! Ahmed Deedat. I watched with interest, though there were no new arguments for Islam (or challenges to Christianity) that I hadn't already run across in my previous studies. They wanted to know what I thought of the debate, if maybe I had any doubts about my faith. I could see their disappointment when I said no and thanked them for helping me understand the issues better. On my following visit, we ate another meal very similar to the last one at Ahmed's apartment and talked earnestly about our religious differences for several hours.

Our conversation ended on a strained but still somewhat friendly note when, after I had explained to them at length why I believe Jesus is God, Ahmed informed me that they did not really want to hear about that. They wanted very much to convince me that not only is Jesus *not* God (though they do revere him as a prophet), but also that I should abandon Christianity and become Muslim.

"That I could never do, my friends," I said with a smile. But it was clear that their patience with me was nearing its end. "Why do you keep coming back here?" one of them asked me, genuinely puzzled at my persistence.

Knowing I needed some kind of pretext for continuing my visits to the mosque, I enrolled in Arabic classes, but I sensed that Ahmed saw that as a contrivance. One evening as we were walking out to the parking lot, he stopped and looked at me closely, his brow furrowed. "The imam is becoming concerned about your visits," he said. "He wonders why you keep coming back even though you don't show any signs of embracing Islam."

"I'm sincerely trying to learn," I responded. "Is that a problem?"

"I want to ask you a direct question," he replied. "And I hope you will give me a direct answer." I nodded.

"Are you an F.B.I. agent?"

"What?!" I exclaimed with a laugh. "No, of course I'm not from the F.B.I. I'm just a guy with questions." But it was clear from the look in his eye that he wasn't entirely convinced.

"There is some concern that maybe you have been trying to gather information."

"I assure you that that's definitely not the case, Ahmed. I just want to know more about your religion."

And though that was my last visit to the mosque, I did learn a great deal from the experience—things that have helped me over the years since then to be respectful and understanding whenever I've had a chance to talk about Jesus with Muslims. But it also taught me how important it is for all Christians to really *know* Jesus Christ, to know who he is and why he died for our sins. To understand that he is true God and true man and that no argument or objection raised against these truths will ever disprove them. In short, my visits to the mosque helped me become a better, more convinced Christian.

———————•••••◆————•••

"For though I am free from all men, I have made myself a slave to all, that I might win the more. To the Jews I became as a Jew, in order to win Jews; to those under the law I became as one under the law—though not being myself under the law—that I might win those under the law. To those outside the law I became as one outside the law—not being without law toward God but under the law of Christ—that I might win those outside the law. To the weak I became weak, that I might win the weak. I have become all things to all men, that I might by all means save some" (1 Cor 9:19–22).

Chapter 28

An Embarrassing Case of Mistaken Sacramental Identity

ONE SATURDAY, many years ago, a friend of mine visited from out of town. Looking for some prayerful encouragement and, probably, a kick in the rear to get himself to confession, he confided painfully to me that he had fallen into a pattern of sexual sin, about which he was understandably distressed and embarrassed. (Let's just say that the particular sins burdening him went beyond the solitary sort that many men are prone to these days.)

During a frank conversation in which my friend was searingly honest with himself, I offered some advice and encouragement, after which we clambered into my car and drove to a nearby parish so he could receive the Sacrament of Penance.

His discomfiture at having to confess these sins to another man was palpable.

Promising him the meager benefit of my prayers for courage and trust in the Lord's mercy, I knelt in a pew at the back of the church while my friend approached the confessional.

The red light above the door indicated that a priest was waiting for penitents. Aside from my friend and me, the church was completely empty.

Fifteen minutes pass. My friend exited the confessional and scuttled to a back pew in the shadows of the left transept, where he remained motionless in prayer, head bowed, his face covered by remorseful hands.

There were no other penitents.

Five more minutes went by.

The priest exited the confessional and walked toward the back of the church . . . where I happened to be kneeling.

The priest did not notice my friend kneeling in the transept.

The priest did, however, notice me.

The closer he got, the more clearly I saw the abashed look on his face as he recognized me.

Although this priest and I had only ever exchanged but a few words in passing, he knew who I was.

Awkward is not a sufficiently descriptive adjective to describe the look we exchanged as he passed by. Panicking, I realized the priest thought he had just heard my confession.

"Oh, ho!" I imagined the good priest thinking to himself. "What a fraud!"

Meanwhile, my friend remained conveniently engrossed in prayer for several minutes more, off in his wonderfully anonymous dark corner, unaware of the unpleasant little drama playing out as the priest whisked by me with that look on his face.

I admit, I was tempted to run after him and explain that he had it all wrong, that I am not that guy, that his new-found view of me was really just a case of mistaken identity. But I stayed put.

Why? Because, in a momentary flash of (albeit dim) understanding, I was painfully reminded of my own lifetime-constructed ziggurat of sin and that my savior, Jesus Christ, was wrongly accused of crimes he did not commit but willingly suffered their penalty—for my sake. For my countless sins, he suffered so that by his stripes I may be healed.

In the years that have passed since that day, I occasionally see that priest. In truth, I have searched for but never detected even a hint of "that look" on his face when he sees me. Perhaps he forgot what he heard in the confessional minutes later (many priests have assured me that this happens to them—a kind of vocational grace that enables them to blank out any lingering memories of what is unburdened to them by penitents). Or maybe he is just a kind and compassionate man who would never even think of betraying the thought that he had been scandalized. I don't know.

I do know this though: My sins may be different from my friend's, or yours, or that priest's, but I am a sinner in grievous need of God's grace and mercy, just like my friend. Just like you. And I am so grateful to the Lord for his gift of the Sacrament of Penance. He knows how much and how often I need it.[1]

"Have no anxiety about anything, but in everything by prayer and supplication with thanksgiving let your requests be made known to God. And the peace of God, which surpasses all understanding, will guard your hearts and your minds in Christ Jesus" (Phil 4:6–7).

---

[1] NB: A slightly edited version of this appeared in my 2012 book *Envoy for Christ* (Servant).

Chapter 29

Do the Right Thing

TEMPTATIONS COME in different forms. Some are brassy and exotic, hawking their wares so loudly that we can't easily ignore them. Others creep up quietly and, in whispers, coax us ever so gently toward a bad decision. We might hardly realize the temptation is there until, ZAP! We've given in, and it's too late.

Being human, we're all afflicted with temptations. Being Catholic, we have some powerful prayers and sacramental defenses against them.

I recently went through a moment of temptation that, as I look back on it, taught me an important lesson. I had been contacted by a Catholic publishing company with a request to rent my mailing list. (That kind of request is always nice, since it represents revenue. In this instance, the company wanted to rent the entire list.)

The request was accompanied by a sample of the mailing they intended to send to the list: a catalogue of books on spirituality and prayer written by a priest I was unfamiliar with. Although I had never read anything by the priest, something told me there might be a problem with his work. A little bell started ringing in the back of my mind, a warning that I should look more deeply into this before I allowed the list to be rented.

But no, I thought. I can just put this nagging question out of my mind and not ask any questions. Ignorance is bliss, right? Wrong. I knew that as tempting as it was to keep my mouth shut and not ask any questions that could bring answers I might not like, if I suppressed my conscience just long enough to make a few bucks, I'd kick myself later. It would be better to find out for sure if this writer was okay.

So, I got on the horn and called a priest I knew from the same order as the priest whose books were listed in the catalogue.

"Father," I began, "What can you tell me about the writings of a priest named Fr. N?" His groan told the whole story. "No. His stuff isn't good at all. His books have a lot of problems with syncretism [i.e., mixing Catholicism with, in this particular case, Hinduism]," the priest said. "I'd stay away from it."

"That's what I needed to know," I said and hung up after thanking him for taking a moment to help me out.

But to be doubly sure, I called a second and then a third priest to get their corroboration. They, too, panned the books in the catalogue. So, armed with that information, I contacted the list rental agent and told him we couldn't approve the rental request from that publishing company.

The revenue from that rental would have been nice, but I knew I had an obligation to the folks on our list not to knowingly allow bad material to be sent to them. And this is where the temptation slithered into the picture.

I soon received a call from the director of the publishing company—a pleasant and well-spoken gentleman—asking me to reconsider. He did his best to reassure me that the writings in that catalogue were sound and that, although some had criticized the author, he really was a respected and important authority on spirituality. I have no doubt that the man was being sincere and that he really believed what he was saying was true. And, to be honest, I began to waver.

An image of the tidy check that would be sent in payment for that list rental floated up before my eyes. Mmm, yes. It really wasn't a big deal after all, *was* it? I mean, come on, his books were teaching people how to pray, and that's a good thing, right? What harm would there be in relenting and allowing the list to be rented?

I lulled on that way for a few moments, coming very close to giving in to the temptation, before I snapped out of it. No, it wouldn't be right to do this, I reminded myself, regardless of the money.

So, before I had a chance to change my mind and lapse back into my cowardly, greedy ways, I said a final no and thanked the director of the publishing company for calling to check, and hung up the phone.

About a week later I was stunned to read a story that went out on the religion wire services. It was about how the Vatican had formally, publicly condemned the writings of a priest—the exact same priest whose book catalogue I had declined. It was uncomfortable to think how close I had come to giving in and allowing the folks on the list to receive bad materials, all because I was tempted to take the money and look the other way.

Was this statement by the Vatican God's way of getting my attention? Perhaps, but regardless, he got it in a big way. If I had been stupid enough and greedy enough (and I hate to admit it, but I very nearly was) to suspend my ethics and look the other way on that list rental deal, I would have had to apologize to the many people on the list who would have received the mailing. It was unsettling to realize how close I had come to letting that happen.

The lesson learned is simple but crucial: we have to do the right thing. If we don't, we'll be miserable and our bad choices will let other people down. Ultimately, our true happiness hinges on how readily we strive to do the right thing rather than the easy thing.

Ironically, it seems to be an axiomatic rule of the universe that doing what's right is usually not easy. Life is filled with opportunities to look the other way, to cheat just a bit here or there, to remain quiet when we should speak up about a mistake we made, to let money dictate the boundaries and test the elasticity of our business ethics.

The fact that we're Catholics is itself no guarantee that we'll always behave as Catholics in our business dealings. That's why we have to stay close to Christ in the sacraments, especially Penance. Any of us could fill volumes with examples from our own lives of temptations we've encountered in the sphere of business, and we might take satisfaction in knowing we conquered (or at least ignored) most of them.

But I do know this much: some temptations are overt and others are subtle, but all of them can be dangerous. This is why St. Peter warned us, "Be sober and vigilant. Your opponent the devil is prowling around like a roaring lion looking for [someone] to devour. Resist him, steadfast in faith, knowing that your fellow believers throughout the world undergo the same sufferings" (1 Pt 5:8–9, NABRE).

Let's not be discouraged or apprehensive. That dark thundercloud of warning has a silver lining: "The God of all grace who called you to his eternal glory through Christ [Jesus] will himself restore, confirm, strengthen, and establish you after you have suffered a little. To him be dominion forever. Amen" (1 Pt 5:10–11, NABRE). Amen.[1]

"The Lord is faithful; he will strengthen you and guard you from evil" (2 Thes 3:3).

---

[1] NB: This also appeared in my 2012 book *Envoy for Christ* (Servant).

Chapter 30

The Napkin

STANDING IN line to pay for some copies at a quick print shop, I noticed a sign on the wall behind the cash register:

WHAT I IF TOLD YOU THAT

YOU THIS READ WRONG?

My subconscious mind thought it said something slightly different from what it actually said. (It took you a moment to realize it, too, right?) That sign is a reminder of how sometimes we misinterpret even simple messages. Such misunderstandings can be minor and insignificant or they can be major and serious, but they inevitably result in a distorted view of the facts, and that's never a good thing. I've learned this the hard way more than a few times in my life.

Sometimes we think we see things that just aren't there. This happens more often than you might think. There's even a technical name for it: *pareidolia*—the mind's tendency to impose meaning and significance on purely random collections of things, for example, seeing shapes or faces in clouds.

Examples of this have cropped up in recent years, sometimes making the evening news: people seeing images of the Virgin Mary in the bark of a tree or the face of Jesus on a piece of toast. Granted, sometimes the shape of a cloud or the gnarled bark of a tree can indeed look surprisingly like a face or an angel or the Virgin Mary, but it would be safe to say that, almost always, these phenomena are just striking examples of pareidolia and nothing more. The fact that everyone, at one time or another, *sees* something that isn't really there, is sufficient evidence that it's not uncommon for people to impose incorrect meaning on things.

I found that this happens frequently with the Bible when a sincere believer *sees* in its pages a doctrine the Bible doesn't actually teach. Examples include the Protestant principles of *sola scriptura* (Latin for "by Scripture alone," or more colloquially, "the Bible only") and *sola fide* ([justification] Latin for "by faith alone"), neither of which are found in the Bible but are, in fact, explicitly denied by the Bible.

Sometimes we see things that are there and are not random, but we misunderstand their meaning nonetheless due to some ambiguity. The following statement is a case in point:

Time flies like the wind. Fruit flies like bananas.

This oddball phrase is what linguistics experts call an *antanaclasis*, a form of amphiboly, which is an equivocal statement in which one word carries two different meanings in the same sentence. Here, "flies" is used both as a verb and as a noun. But if you didn't understand this ambiguity or, if someone didn't explain it, the subtle meaning might be lost on you, and you'd likely write it off as gibberish. At the very least, you would misunderstand what was being said. Brandeis University professor, David Hackett Fischer, blames the problem of *semantical ambiguity* as a common cause of misunderstanding the facts of history.

If it's possible to misread a simple sentence like the one above, it's far more possible, even likely, to misread and therefore misunderstand the complexities of history. This is equally true, I have found, with the Bible. Some go astray when they read into the Bible something that's not really there (*eisegesis*) and others when they ignore something in the Bible that doesn't fit with their own theories and preferences. I learned this lesson in a particularly vivid way years ago when, after finishing a parish apologetics seminar, two men—both Calvinists—approached me asking if I'd give them the opportunity to show me how wrong I was in my understanding of the Bible.

We headed to a nearby Denny's where they launched into a series of objections to Catholic Marian doctrines, informing me that the Catholic Church teaches things "that are not in the Bible." But when I opened my Bible and began quoting passages that pertain to those doctrines, they suddenly switched from "that's not in the Bible" argument to "you're taking that out of context." When I wouldn't back down, things started getting tense.

"You're misunderstanding that verse!" they said. "That's not what it means."

"No," I countered, "I understand its meaning just fine. You guys are taking it out of context."

"No, we understand it correctly. You don't."

"No, I understand it correctly. You don't."

And so it went. For the better part of a very frustrating and unproductive hour of bickering—the classic Mexican standoff where neither side backs down. The two Calvinists were adamant that none of the biblical passages I raised could possibly be understood in a way that might favor the Catholic Church's teachings about Mary. They simply would not budge on that position.

So, when it became clear that this conversation was going nowhere, and I was just about to thank them and leave, I had an idea. "What do I have to lose?" I asked myself.

Nothing I've said thus far has had any positive affect on this conversation, so I might as well give this a try. Couldn't hurt.

Grabbing a napkin, I jotted down the following words and pushed it across the table toward them. I wrote: "I NEVER SAID YOU STOLE MONEY."

"Do you guys understand what I mean by this statement?" I asked.

"Sure," the guy on the left said, glancing down and then back to me.

"Are you sure you understand it?"

"Yes, I'm sure I understand it. 'I never said you stole money.' No big deal. What's your point?"

Seeing this irritated them both, I pressed yet again, asking if he was quite sure he understood what I meant by those six words.

"Yes! I do! What's your point?" he retorted in exasperation.

"*Wellll*, what if I meant: '*I* never said you stole money'? implying that someone else said it. "Or did I mean: 'I never *said* you stole money.' I thought it, but I didn't say it. Or maybe I meant: 'I never said *you* stole money.' Someone else did. Or did I have in mind that 'I never said you *stole* money'? Maybe you lost it or you accidentally set it on fire, but you didn't steal it. Or did I mean: 'I never said you stole *money*,' implying that you stole something else?"

It was clear from the look on their faces that I had scored a point. I could see the lightbulb above their heads turn on. They glanced at each other sheepishly, and one said, "Well, alright, if you put it that way, I guess we can't be sure exactly what you meant by that."

"Alright, fellas," I smiled. "That's my point. If you can't be certain (as you've admitted) that you understand accurately the meaning of the six words I just wrote down in your presence, what makes you so sure you are automatically guaranteed to understand every passage of the Bible? What makes you so sure that your understanding of the verses we've discussed here tonight is correct and mine is wrong? I mean, really. If (as you admit) you can't be sure you know what I mean by what I wrote on that napkin, then why are you so absolutely sure you understand all seventy-three books of the Bible, written by different authors, in different languages, at different times, for different audiences, and for different purposes?"

It was then that our conversation pretty much ground to a halt. I had made my point, and there wasn't much else to say, so we shook hands and went our separate ways.

I had learned a new technique for finding a way through the Bible-badminton impasse that often arises when Catholics and Protestants get into doctrinal disagreements, and I've used it countless times since then.

Oh, and there was a happy ending to that conversation with the two Calvinists. About six months later, at another parish speaking event, one of those two guys (the ex-Catholic) was there. He bee-lined over to me and said with a grin, "Hey, do you remember me?"

"I sure do!" I replied, feigning enthusiasm, though actually I wasn't all that pleased to see him again. I figured he wanted round two with me. Turns out he didn't.

"Do you remember that napkin thing you showed us when we met at Denny's awhile back?"

"Of course."

"Well, that's what started me on the road back to the Catholic Church," he said with an even wider grin. "I'm back in the Catholic Church!" He explained that though the "napkin thing" I did that evening didn't in itself change his mind, it did act as a kind of key that unlocked the mental door that had slammed shut against the Catholic Church at some time in his past. He began reading the Church Fathers and saw how their understanding of the Bible tracked with those teachings of the Catholic Church he had thought were erroneous, and it wasn't long before he put two-and-two together and realized the reason why the teaching of the Fathers and other early Christians coincided so identically with the Catholic Church: because they themselves *were* Catholic.

"There is a way which seems right to a man,
    but its end is the way to death" (Prv 16:25).

"He who states his case first seems right,
    until the other comes and examines him" (Prv 18:17).

"First of all you must understand this, that no prophecy of scripture is a matter of one's own interpretation, because no prophecy ever came by the impulse of man, but men moved by the Holy Spirit spoke from God" (2 Pt 1:20–21).

"Our beloved brother Paul wrote to you according to the wisdom given him, speaking of this as he does in all his letters. There are some things in them hard to understand, which the ignorant and unstable twist to their own destruction, as they do the other scriptures" (2 Pt 3:15–16).

Chapter 31

My Christmas Surprise

THE FIRST dozen years of our marriage were financially tight for Nancy and me. Nine months and three weeks after our wedding, our first child, a boy, arrived. And God in His generosity continued to bless us with more children (a total of six boys and five girls) about every two years or so after that.

We were happy and grateful for each new son and daughter who made an appearance, even though many of our friends, and even some family members, weren't enthusiastic or even pleased by the fact that we were having so many children. No matter. My wife and I were both willing to accept however many gifts of new life the Lord might want to send us, and time rolled along faster and faster as each new member of our family came along.

It was kind of weird for us back in those early days of child-rearing. I mean, on the one hand, we weren't the least bit afraid of declaring our *openness to life* each time Nancy's belly began to swell with the promise of another son or daughter on the way. Yet we were met with various careless, and sometimes untoward, comments from strangers and even friends, especially when Nancy went into the store pushing a stroller with four or five kids in tow, *and* visibly pregnant with the next one.

"Are you done now?" "Was this one a mistake?" "Do you know what causes that?" "Don't you have a TV?" Etc. We've heard them all. (My favorite rejoinder to that last inquiry was: *"If you prefer TV to what causes this, then you're doing something wrong."*)

Shortly after baby number three was born, Nancy and I were able to scrape enough money together to afford the down payment on a modest home of our own, just 1,165 square feet. Our first! Seven years later, we had a total of seven children, stacked like firewood, in our three-bedroom house. In many ways, that phase of life was one of our very best. We had no money, but we had each other. Nancy worked hard, devotedly, and lovingly as a stay-at-home mom, while I commuted to my job, working long hours to make ends meet. And so they did.

God always seemed to provide. And with each new mouth to feed, a pay raise in my salary always seemed to materialize, as did countless other just-in-the-nick-of-time blessings of food, clothing, and various necessities whose urgent need were met inevitably by the benevolence of others who, uncannily, seemed to be moved to do something kind for us always at just the right time.

In my own eyes, I was selfless and welcoming to others. But the Lord showed me otherwise one particular Christmas when he bulldozed my myopic self-assurance that I was *generous.*

Through a series of unfortunate events, my parents went bankrupt earlier that year. My youngest four siblings were still at home. My folks had nowhere else to go and no money to find a new home, so Nancy and I invited them to move into our already crowded house. We made the best of it, all fifteen of us crammed (more or less cheerfully) into our microscopic 1,165 square foot home. The fact that Christmas was upon us, honestly, didn't make things any easier.

Some background: In the mid-1970s, shortly after the fall of Saigon, my parents generously sponsored a Vietnamese family to come live in our home for over a year. With a large family of their own, it was a sacrifice, but it worked out well and we were all happy—two different races, cultures, languages, and customs blending under one roof. These dear people, refugees from the horrors they left behind in Vietnam, truly became like family to us. My family and I thus encountered a very different culture, learned to enjoy unfamiliar customs and *delicious* cuisine, and developed new ways to become more open and welcoming, which was the best part. The experience helped us become better Catholics, better people. But some lessons, however powerful, can fade with time.

Years later, when my parents went bankrupt, and I was thrust anew into the situation of welcoming "outsiders" into my home, I'm ashamed to say that I failed the test. I had already swallowed hard and done the right thing regarding my parents and siblings (what else could I do, I reminded myself), but I could and did say no when Christmas brought a new request. My dad informed me that a member of our erstwhile Vietnamese guest family—a young man named Cường—was going to be in the area and had asked to stay with us for Christmas.

As much as I wanted to see Cường again, I just couldn't fathom how we could squeeze yet *another* person (in this case, a fully grown man) into our already alarmingly overcrowded house. I was worried that there wouldn't be enough food, enough room, enough *hot water* for showers! And, truth be told, I must admit that I was secretly worried that there wouldn't be enough of those things for me personally. I'm ashamed to admit that now, but that's the truth.

So I said no. "No, Dad. We just can't do it. I'd like to have Cường over for a visit, and maybe some other time we can do that, but not now. There are just too many people here," I explained, hoping my dad would see it my way and pass along the word that *there was no room at the inn* (*cf.* Lk 2:7) that night.

But then Nancy, my gracious and loving wife, asked me to reconsider. Sure, we literally had no room to offer another house-guest, but we did have a couch. And we could always make a little more food. And was it really *that* big a deal if we ran out of hot water for a while and I had to take a cold shower? She was right, of course, but I balked and stalled and argued for a while, tossing out selfish reasons why I didn't want to welcome him. I was just being selfish.

Eventually, begrudgingly, I acquiesced, ready to resent our new visitor for taking up space in our already thronged home. But as God's grace would have it, as soon as he arrived, it was as if no problem had ever arisen. It was great to see him again, and we all laughed and reminisced and celebrated in a way and to a depth that not only did I not anticipate but which I had never experienced before. It turned out, to my grudging surprise, to be an uproariously fun, happy, and blessed family celebration.

On that cramped and crowded Christmas, the Lord gave me a life-changingly important gift: *himself*. He enlarged my heart. In my selfishness and complacency, I thought I already *had* made room for Jesus. How wrong I was. God's gift to me that Christmas was a deeper understanding of his words: "Behold, I stand at the door and knock; if any one hears my voice and opens the door, I will come in to him and eat with him, and he with me" (Rev 3:20).

———————————•••————◆————•••———————————

"Give, and it will be given to you; good measure, pressed down, shaken together, running over, will be put into your lap. For with the measure you give will be the measure you get back" (Lk 6:38).

"By this we know love, that he laid down his life for us; and we ought to lay down our lives for the brethren. But if anyone has the world's goods and sees his brother in need, yet closes his heart against him, how does God's love abide in him?" (1 Jn 3:16–17).

Chapter 32

The Policeman

A MONG THE people I remember from the parish where
my wife and I were married thirty-five years ago, one
who stands out in my mind was a forty-five-ish policeman.
I don't recall his name and don't think I ever even spoke to
him, but I do remember seeing him every Sunday at Mass and
at the occasional weekday morning Masses I infrequently
attended. I'm told he was a daily Mass-goer.

Picturing the cruciform interior of that little parish church,
I can still see him in my mind's eye sitting with his wife and
children—off to the left and several pews back—just another
Catholic family. Ordinary, yes, but quite memorable, even
after all these years.

What I remember most about the policeman isn't his
appearance or where he sat at Mass, or even the mortifying
sexual scandal that engulfed him once the local paper
printed the bawdy details of a malfeasance he was accused of
committing with a local woman while on duty. It must have
been utterly horrible for him and his family.

The scandal swirled for a while, as scandals do, especially
when they involve someone who by all appearances is
exemplary and upright. No doubt, it was an excruciating
experience for him to endure, and that's what makes him so

memorable. It was what he did during and after the scandal that made a deep impression on me.

As I recall, the policeman lost his job. He also lost his marriage, many friends, and his standing in the community. Word gets around quickly, you know. He may even have come close to losing his faith, but I don't think he did. That's because he didn't stop going to Mass. He didn't check out under the strain of public scrutiny and opprobrium.

Sunday after Sunday, at the height of the scandal and beyond, I saw him at Mass, sitting alone in the same pew he previously occupied with his wife and kids. Sometimes, I saw him sitting alone, sometimes with his teenage daughter at his side. She, apparently, never gave up on her dad.

This beleaguered man, in the midst of a frighteningly turbulent storm, refused to let go of his lifeline to God. All the evidence I needed to know this was true was his dogged persistence in attending Mass where he surely felt parishioners' eyes on him, even if he couldn't quite hear the murmuring mouths of gossip and judgment: *"Yes, that's him over there." "Can you believe it?" "Well, I never." "And he was a* policeman!*"*

Even the profound embarrassment he felt couldn't prevent him from braving that storm head on. I'm certain the Lord sustained him when everything else in his life had collapsed. I wonder sometimes what ever became of him. Did he reunite with his wife? Was he able to get another job in law enforcement? Did he hang in there and stay the course of following Jesus in the Catholic Church? I'll never know how things turned out for him, at least on this side of eternity, but over the years I've offered up prayers of gratitude to the Lord for allowing me to witness this painful episode.

The policeman's crucible, even as I viewed it from a distance, taught me important lessons about clinging to the Lord, especially when sin, failure, and shame close in from all sides. It reminded me that God's grace is more powerful than my sin. And it encouraged me to seek His mercy and forgiveness more fervently whenever I sin through pride and weakness.

The words Psalm 51 ring true in my heart whenever I pause and reflect on this lesson about sin, perseverance, and restoration.

———— •·• ——◆—— •·• ————

"Have mercy on me, O God, according to your merciful
love;
according to your abundant mercy blot out my
transgressions.
Wash me thoroughly from my iniquity,
and cleanse me from my sin!
For I know my transgressions,
and my sin is ever before me.
Against you, you only, have I sinned,
and done that which is evil in your sight,
so that you are justified in your sentence
and blameless in your judgment.
Behold, I was brought forth in iniquity,
and in sin did my mother conceive me.
Behold, you desire truth in the inward being;
therefore teach me wisdom in my secret heart.
Purge me with hyssop, and I shall be clean;
wash me, and I shall be whiter than snow.
Make me hear joy and gladness;
let the bones which you have broken rejoice.

Hide your face from my sins,
    and blot out all my iniquities.
Create in me a clean heart, O God,
    and put a new and right spirit within me"
(Psalm 51:1–10).

Chapter 33

The Scar

WORKING PART-TIME as a short-order cook in the cafeteria of a department store was a great gig for sixteen-year-old me. It was my first real job, and I was raking in a whole $2.35 per hour, enough to fund my modest goals of that era, which largely centered on buying record albums from my favorite bands, a new shirt or a pair of jeans here and there and, when I went out on dates, buying pizza, popcorn, and movie tickets. These goals were in addition to learning the art of cooking patty melts, fish & chips, and cheeseburgers.

I was also responsible for bussing tables, scooping ice-cream, making malts, running the cash register, keeping the ice dispenser topped off, sweeping and mopping, scraping the fry griddle, emptying the deep-fat fryer vats at the end of the day, and washing dishes. The entire end-of-day operation could be handled by two people. I typically worked the 4:00–9:00 evening shift. Once the manager had counted out the drawer and prepared the day's deposit, she usually left for home by 7:00, which meant that one other person and I were responsible for cleaning things up and closing things out.

One employee I worked with regularly was a guy named Arnold. Tall, overweight, and pimply, with a shock of unruly brown hair, Arnold was about my age, fun-loving, and as mature and responsible as I was, which meant that once we had finished our work—and sometimes even before that—we would goof off doing stupid stuff, knowing we wouldn't get caught because the lights in the cafeteria were turned off and we were back in the kitchen where nobody could see us and nobody ever checked on us. Hilarity ensued.

We weren't supposed to leave the cafeteria before 9:00 a.m., so Arnold and I would always try to get everything done as early as possible so we'd have some quality time to sword fight before we left for the day. We didn't have actual *swords*, of course, which I'm pretty sure would have been against company policy (though I never inquired). Instead, we used mop handles, broom handles, and the ice machine shovel, which was about three feet long, made of sturdy PVC plastic, and had a broad flat end, making it the perfect tool to give Arnold a painful whack on the leg or arm. I learned to wield that ice shovel like a samurai short sword.

It's a wonder no one ever ventured back into the kitchen area in search of the source of all the din we made.

My interest in sword fighting came to an abrupt halt one evening when Arnold, who had been swinging and hacking more aggressively than usual, managed to steadily force me back until I had no more room to maneuver. My back was literally to the wall. And he didn't let up. My samurai ice shovel wasn't enough to protect me from the blow that ended our combat.

Aiming the mop handle at me like a medieval knight in a joust, Arnold charged forward and hit me with a hard glancing blow square on the mouth. The blood running down my chin signaled the end of our mischief.

"Yikes!" he muttered, his mop handle slipping from his hand and clattering to the tiled floor. "Hey, I'm really sorry about that, man. Looks like I cut you pretty bad."

"Nah, it's nothing," I said through bloody teeth as I stepped over to the hand sink, splashing water on my face so I could get a look at the wound. "Looks like it's just a cut," I said gamely, feeling with the tip of my tongue to make sure all my teeth were in place.

They were, but when I saw the tip of my tongue *poking clean through the cut below my lower lip,* I got dizzy and had to sit down for a few minutes. The mop handle had cut clean through. This, I realized, would need stitches. But of course, I realized that getting stitches would also necessitate telling my parents what had happened, which I wasn't about to do.

Realizing that the generic "I bumped into something" excuse would never pass muster with my preternaturally inquisitive parents, I latched onto Plan B. I didn't exactly want to *lie* to my folks if I could avoid it, so I decided not to show them the injury and simply said, "I got cut. No big deal."

They bought it. And Band-Aids hid the evidence long enough for the wound to heal. That jagged little scar was all that remained to remind me of my youthful folly.

To this day, some forty years later, whenever I shave or wash my face, I can still see that small disfigurement, and I remember my stupid, juvenile, sword-fighting antics with a twinge of embarrassment and regret. How immature and ridiculous I was then. But it's also a helpful reminder that, no matter how old one gets, it's always possible to lapse into immature and ridiculous behavior if we aren't careful and circumspect.

Which is why, in an analogous sort of way, that scar is good for me. It's an enduring monument to my youthful stupidity, a signpost pointing toward the truth of St. Paul's teaching about Christian maturity and why we all need to stop goofing off and get serious about our life in Christ:

When I was a child, I spoke like a child, I thought like a child, I reasoned like a child; when I became a man, I gave up childish ways. (1 Cor 13:11)

"Brethren, do not be children in your thinking; be infants in evil, but in thinking be mature" (1 Cor 14:20).

Chapter 34

The Jerk

I BECAME an instant Steve Martin fan the day I first heard his newly-released 1977 comedy album, *Let's Get Small.* Listening to it over and over, it wasn't long before I had memorized every line of that bizarre routine, even down to his sardonic cackle and trademark, "*Well, excuuuuuse me!*" (which was the "in" catch-phrase back then). I found his absurdist style of humor wildly hilarious, especially his exaggerated sarcasm, and I quickly adopted it as my own way to be hip and humorous. Turns out, however, that when Steve Martin was sarcastic, people loved it and laughed, but when I mimicked that sarcasm (presuming that I too was being hilarious), I got at best mixed results. I couldn't pull it off like my comedy idol. Worse yet, I didn't *realize* that I wasn't pulling it off. And, that's how I unwittingly became a jerk.

Many uncomfortable and unfortunate memories of that era in my life resurface as I think about the difficulties my big mouth got me into because I had confused sarcasm with genuine humor. Like the time in my freshman year in high school (even before I had discovered Steve Martin) when I made a sarcastic joke about a fat kid in my class. I didn't even know he had overheard it. As I was getting dressed in the locker room, he strode over and, without a word, punched me square in the face as hard as he could, flattening me physically and knocking my pride down several pegs.

Or the time at the Youth Encounter Retreat I went on when I was eighteen. At the very end, all the retreatants were brought into a large hall where our family and friends were waiting to surprise us. Each of us in turn were asked to stand and give a brief testimonial about how the weekend had impacted us spiritually and to say a word of thanks to our "Kris Kringle"—all the retreatants drew names at the beginning and anonymously did little Secret Santa acts of kindness for that person, including writing a heartfelt note of encouragement to him or her.

Turns out my "Kris Kringle" was a sweet girl a year or so younger than me. To this day, I still kick myself for the obnoxious stupidity that came out of my mouth when it was my turn to speak. Smirking, in full-on Steve Martin mode, I chortled, "Wow! I'm sure glad I didn't get someone *ugly!*" Even as I pronounced each stupid syllable, I started kicking myself for saying them.

Instead of amused chuckles and admiring "this guy is really hilarious" expressions from the audience, many groaned in disappointment and irritation. Several gasped audibly. Glancing around, I saw more than a few furrowed brows and heads shaking in shocked disapproval at my exceedingly not-funny sarcasm. "*What a jerk,*" many, I'm sure, were thinking. I sat down quickly, ashamed and angry at myself for—once again!—being boorish and impertinent when all I really intended was to be funny and likeable.

Or those times on the job (there were several) when I thought I was being oh-so-clever with my oh-so-sarcastic wisecracks that offended co-workers to the point where one even quit her part-time job rather than have to work with me. Seriously. The retail store we worked at was having a routine financial audit performed one day, and one of the cashiers, a thirty-ish woman, wondered aloud if the auditors might want to question her and the other cashiers as part of the process. The possibility of this happening didn't seem to particularly bother her, so I don't think she had a guilty conscience. In fact, she seemed to be a perfectly honest and upright person.

Ever ready to make a joke, I popped off with some snappy comment about how, "If you're honest and not stealing from the till"—here I pantomimed a wink-wink, nudge-nudge gesture, suggesting that maybe she *was* stealing—"then you've got nothing to worry about." The offended glance she shot me wasn't the reaction I had expected. Later that day, I asked the manager where she was, as I hadn't seen her around. "She quit," he said with a look of frustration. "She didn't say why. She just quit." Well, *I* knew why and didn't volunteer that information.

There are other similar examples of when I came across like a jerk because of my misguided attempts at humor. But I'm actually glad I can't remember the specifics any more. But the details are no longer important. What's important is that I was able to unlearn that bad old habit of misusing cutting sarcasm in an attempt to be funny. I had embarrassed and alienated people, hurt their feelings, and made myself look like a idiot, all because I didn't control my tongue.

I'm very sorry for that and for all the ways I offended people when I was crass and conceited and uncareful. Thankfully, by God's grace and some friends who cared enough about me to give a gentle but well-placed rebuke when I needed it, I outgrew and abandoned my sophomoric, gimmicky penchant for Steve Martin-esque humor.

Steve Martin's 1979 movie *The Jerk* will always be for me more than just an amusing move. The title has a special meaning and is a reminder that I should leave being a wild-and-crazy-guy to professionals like him.

———— ••• ———— ◆ ———— ••• ————

*"He who keeps his mouth and his tongue
    keeps himself out of trouble"* (Prv 21:23).

*"Set a guard, over my mouth, O LORD;
    keep watch over the door of my lips!"* (Ps 141:3).

*"For we all make many mistakes, and if any one makes
no mistakes in what he says he is a perfect man, able to
bridle the whole body also. If we put bits into the mouths
of horses that they may obey us, we guide their whole
bodies. Look at the ships also; though they are so great
and are driven by strong winds, they are guided by a very
small rudder wherever the will of the pilot directs. So the
tongue is a little member and boasts of great things. How
great a forest is set ablaze by a small fire! And the tongue
is a fire. The tongue is an unrighteous world among our
members, staining the whole body, setting on fire the
cycle of nature, and set on fire by hell. For every kind of
beast and bird, of reptile and sea creature, can be tamed
and has been tamed by humankind, but no human
being can tame the tongue—a restless evil, full of deadly
poison. With it we bless the Lord and Father, and with it
we curse men, who are made in the likeness of God. From
the same mouth come blessing and cursing. My brethren,
this ought not to be so"* (Jas 3:2–10).

Chapter 35

The Beehive

IN THE early 1970s, my dad had a rather peculiar coworker whom I'll call Rich. Short, stocky, and bespectacled, Rich looked and acted a lot like the bumbling dad character played by Rick Moranis in *Honey, I Shrunk the Kids*. He was friendly and talkative, and quirky, and that made him interesting. I appreciated our conversations partly because he had lots of ideas and theories about life and partly because he was willing to shoot the breeze with adolescent me about pretty much any serious topic, from science to religion. I don't remember many other adults being willing to meet me at my level without talking down to me.

I wondered how Rich and my dad had become friends, given how unalike they were. My dad was always a sharp-dressed man. With polished wingtip shoes, starched white dress shirt, jacket and tie, he went to work each morning looking as if he had just stepped out of the men's suit section of the JC Penny catalogue. That was definitely not the look Rich was going for. It seems he was aiming for the bedraggled look. I never saw him without a plastic pocket-protector in his shirt pocket, loaded with pens. His scientific calculator, ever at the ready, was strapped to his belt like a twentieth century six-shooter, and the duct tape holding his glasses together added a certain flourish to his free and easy, ill-fitting unkemptness.

Working for the same tech company, Rich and my dad sometimes carpooled together, which I guess is how they struck up a friendship. That and the fact that Rich and his wife and kids attended the same parish we did, so we saw them regularly at Sunday Mass and at other parish events. I remember that detail about Rich more than any other: he was a devout, knowledgeable Catholic who really loved the Church. But he was unsophisticated and sincere in a way that made him seem naïve. His was a curious mix of personality traits I'd never run across before.

Rich's most prominent trait by far was procrastination. He routinely put off unpleasant or bothersome things and focused on stuff he enjoyed. This is a common human tendency, of course—a failing most of us are prone to a greater or lesser degree—but Rich had developed it into an art form. He never fixed anything if he absolutely didn't have to and could find a work-around or a step-around. It's difficult to exaggerate the dismal conditions his inveterate procrastination inflicted on his wife and kids.

Although Rich didn't strike me as a bona fide hoarder, he was content to live in an indoor wilderness of boxes and bags of stuff piled up everywhere. His garage was a nightmare cave of cardboard-box stalagmites. Stacks of old newspapers, heaps of half-empty paint cans, broken down appliances (that he assured his long-suffering wife he'd get around to fixing someday), and derelict piles of the random detritus of his life of procrastination made his garage an impenetrable fortress of squalor. Regardless of the weather, his cars were permanently parked in the driveway.

Inside his home, things weren't much better. Countless household repairs went endlessly unattended to because he simply ignored them: from drippy faucets and burned out lightbulbs to broken cupboard handles. Unpatched dings, dents, and holes in the wall were everywhere. The staircase was a cascade of filth, mainly boxes and stacks of stuff he planned to work on someday. Most surprising to me was that afternoon I stopped by their house to deliver something for my mom to find their house was sweltering.

"Why don't you turn on the air-conditioner?" I asked Rich, astonished that they could tolerate the sultry summer heat.

"Can't," he grinned sheepishly. "It broke down awhile back and I haven't had a chance to fix it."

Turns out, as his understandably irritated wife told me when Rich was out of earshot, the AC had gone kaput *two months* earlier! They'd been enduring the heat with the help of a couple of oscillating fans. Mercifully for her and the kids, she was able to prevail upon her husband to call a repair man when the heat had gotten too oppressive and she was no longer willing to wait for him to get around to it. Why his poor wife didn't put her foot down about the rest of the neglect and demand that Rich do *something* to clean things up, I will never know. All I know is that's how they lived. And all because Rich was a big-time, blue-chip, major-league procrastinator. He couldn't be bothered, and everyone around him suffered as a result.

And that brings me to Rich's beehive.

Rich became a reluctant beekeeper when a small crack in the exterior stucco of his house began to attract honey bees. Though it would have taken him less than a minute to patch the breach with a dollop of spackle, Rich never bothered to do so. Once his kids, using sticks, had widened the crack into a solver-dollar sized hole, some enterprising honey bees discovered their new home. You could see them buzzing around that end of the house, and Rich and his family simply stayed out of that corner of their yard. Weeks passed. One day, I stopped by their house on another errand for my mom and found Rich in a state of mild panic about the bees.

"Come here! You've got to see this!" he said, flustered.

Expecting we'd go around to the backyard to see what mischief the bees had gotten up to, he instead beckoned me inside and down the hall toward one of the back bedrooms.

"Careful," he warned as he slowly opened the door to the bedroom and then quickly shut it again. There were *hundreds* of honeybees in there—maybe a thousand. It was incredible. You could hear the dull buzzing of the excited insects through the door. It was frightening.

"My gosh!" I exclaimed. "Has anyone been stung? What are you going to *do*?" I asked incredulously. I couldn't believe he had let things go so long. And that's when, to my gobsmacked, jaw-dropping amazement, I realized just how completely a lifetime of procrastination had paralyzed Rich's ability to confront and resolve problems, even a potentially life-threatening problem like *hundreds of honey bees swarming inside his house.*

"I don't want to get hurt," he said. "I'm not going in there. I tried and they practically attacked me! And I tried covering the hole outside but the bees went crazy and wouldn't let me near it. So I'm just going to . . ."

"Call an exterminator! Right?" I said, more as a command than a question.

"No." Rich said with an air of resignation. "We probably can't afford that. And who knows if they'll need to tent the house like they do with termites. We definitely couldn't afford *that*."

"So . . . what are you going to do then?" I asked, uncomfortable from the angry insectile buzzing just on the other side of the door.

I will never forget his next words, uttered in complete seriousness and abject defeat.

"Well, I'm just going to seal off this room until they go away or die."

Seriously. He actually said that. Worse still, he actually meant it. I was dumbfounded. Rich was actually planning to cede over to a colony of honey bees a whole room of his house. Anything to avoid dealing with the problem. And he did, in fact, seal the door with duct tape and warned his kids sternly to "never go in there." Well, that deal lasted about a week. His wife, poor thing, got stung by a few bees that had infiltrated the kitchen through an non-duct-taped air duct (no-doubt scouting out new rooms for their expansion). This time, she put her foot down hard and Rich reluctantly called an exterminator.

I can't say that Rich's story ended happily ever after. How could it have, given his inability to knuckle down and take care of business? But as for me, I learned a valuable life-lesson about the dangers of procrastination, one that I've had occasion to recall many times over the years since that weird afternoon when I saw just how out-of-control things can get when you put things off.

———————◆———————

"He dies for lack of discipline
and because of his great folly he is lost" (Prv 5:23).

"I passed by the field of a sluggard,
by the vineyard of a man without sense;
and behold, it was all overgrown with thorns;
the ground was covered with nettles,
and its stone wall was broken down.

Then I saw and considered it;
     I looked and received instruction.
A little sleep, a little slumber,
     a little folding of the hands to rest,
and poverty will come upon you like a robber,
     and want like an armed man" (Prv 24:30–34).

"I can do all things in him who strengthens me"
(Phil 4:13).

"Whoever knows what is right to do and fails to do it, for him it is sin" (Jas 4:17).

Chapter 36

The Atheist Lady

I WAS about five-years-old when I discovered, to my childlike astonishment, that not everyone in the world is Catholic. It seemed inconceivable to me that other people wouldn't believe the things that I had been taught by my parents were true. I accepted it as true on face value that Jesus was truly present in the Holy Eucharist at Mass—what looked like a simple disc of bread both before and after the priest elevated it at the Consecration was actually His Body, Blood, Soul, and Divinity—that Mary and all the angels and saints are up in Heaven praying for us to love God, live good lives, and get up there to Heaven with them, that Catholic priests have the power to forgive sins in Jesus's name, and that I should genuflect reverently in front of the tabernacle because God Himself is inside!

These and everything else my parents taught me about God and the Church were evidently true to me because why would my parents who love me lie to me about such weighty matters? It never entered my mind to question my parents about these matters, much less demand proof in support of them before I would acquiesce to believe.

The bursting of the bubble of my childlike faith was mild compared to the jolt I received a few years later when, for the first time, an atheist challenged me about my belief in God.

This happened in 1971. I was eleven, and the atheist, a thirty-something housewife who lived across the street agreed to do my mom a favor and drive my younger sister and me somewhere for her. Improbably, I mentioned "God" along the way, and that's when the fireworks flared.

"*God?* she snorted. "You believe in God, eh?"

My heart started pounding. I had never heard anything like *that* before (certainly not from an *adult*). Glancing up at the rearview mirror, I saw contempt on her face that matched the irritation in her voice.

"Yes . . ." I answered timidly, "I do believe in God."

"Well, there's no such *thing* as God," she snapped. "He doesn't exist, and people who believe in God believe in a myth—a fairy tale."

Well, this irritated *me*. And though I knew I was taking a risk by talking back to an adult, I blurted, "That's ridiculous. God does *too* exist!"

And that's when she shut me down. Hard.

"Have you ever seen any *proof* that God exists?" she sneered into the rearview mirror. "Hmph! Of course you haven't. God is a fairy tale, like Santa Claus or the Easter Bunny. You don't believe *they're* real anymore, do you?"

I glanced nervously at my little sister who *did* still believe in both of the above named fictitious personages. All I could stammer in response to her staccato barrage of anti-God sloganeering were a few wobbly "Yes, God *does* exist" retorts.

She clobbered me with a spate of one-two punches, demanding evidence I didn't have for God's existence and furnishing her own "evidence" that God doesn't, in fact, can't, exist.

War, violence, cancer, and countless other evils exist, she explained, so how could an allegedly all-knowing, all-powerful, all-loving God exist? If He's real, why doesn't He step in and stop these evils?

Of course, as an eleven-year-old pipsqueak, I had zero answers to her arguments and so I rode in embarrassed (and angry) silence for the rest of the ride. That was my introduction to atheism. Yay.

The experience made a lasting impression on me, and over the forty-five years since that day, I've learned a great deal about the irrationality and many internal contradictions of atheism. As an adult, I began to study the profound rational proofs for the existence of God, proofs I had no inkling even existed when I was eleven and trapped in the back seat of Atheist Lady's car. Which is why I'm glad she did what she did. Who knows? If Atheist Lady hadn't hammered me with all those questions about God all those years ago, maybe I wouldn't have felt compelled to find the answers.

As I said in a book I co-authored on this subject, "Ah, if only I could go back in time! Knowing what I know now, were I to have another conversation with Atheist Lady, I believe things would play out rather differently."[1]

—————————————◆—————————————

"For I am not ashamed of the gospel: it is the power of God for salvation to every one who has faith, to the Jew first and also to the Greek. For in it the righteousness of God is revealed through faith for faith; as it is written, "He who through faith is righteous shall live." For the wrath of God is revealed from heaven against all ungodliness and wickedness of men who by their wickedness suppress

[1] Patrick Madrid and Kenneth Hensley, *The Godless Delusion: A Catholic Challenge to Modern Atheism* (Huntington, IN: Our Sunday Visitor, 2010).

the truth. For what can be known about God is plain to them, because God has shown it to them. Ever since the creation of the world his invisible nature, namely, his eternal power and deity, has been clearly perceived in the things that have been made. So they are without excuse; for although they knew God they did not honor him as God or give thanks to him, but they became futile in their thinking and their senseless minds were darkened" (Rom 1:16–21).

Chapter 37

You Have How Many *Kids?*

STANDING IN a checkout line with a friend, waiting to pay for stuff, I happened to mention aloud how many children I had. At that time, I think we *only* had nine. No sooner had I said it than the middle-aged woman standing ahead of me whirled around and snarled, "You have *how many* kids?!" Glaring at me in shocked (shocked!) dismay, it was as if I had just shouted out her social security number or asked how much she weighed.

"Uh, as a matter of fact, my wife and I have nine children," I responded, taken aback by her vehemence. "Do you have a *problem* with that?"

"Yeah, as a matter of fact, I *do* have a problem with that," she hissed through clenched teeth. "All those kids? That's the most selfish thing I've ever heard of!"

"And why is *that*?" I asked crisply, rankled by her rudeness. My wife and I foregoing expensive vacations and nice cars so we could instead shell out for diapers, food, shoes clothes, and an education for our kids, not to mention occasionally having to drag ourselves out of bed at 2:00 in the morning to clean up after a vomiting toddler, sick with the flu, didn't exactly strike me as *selfish*. Turns out, that's not what she meant.

"It's selfish," she scowled, "because you're crowding an already overcrowded planet, you're consuming precious resources, and you're contributing to global warming. You don't *need* that many kids. It's *irresponsible* to have that many kids. It's wrong! It's immoral!"

As I was about to retort, she let fly another broadside: "And I'll bet you're anti-*abortion*, aren't you?!" At this, my friend and I started laughing; clearly not the reaction she had expected.

"Yes, of *course* I'm anti-abortion," I chortled. "What was your first clue, huh? The fact that I have nine kids?"

"I figured," she glared at me acidly. "Well, you'd better get over it. Abortion is legal."

"So what?" I said. "Just because it's legal doesn't mean it's moral. Abortion is . . ."

Before I could finish, she cut me off. "It wouldn't *be* legal if it weren't moral!" she snapped.

And that's when it clicked in my mind how I should proceed. To my delight, this woman had just boxed herself into an untenable position from which to argue.

"Is that so?" I asked, eyebrows arched. "You realize, of course, that *slavery* used to be legal here in the United States, right? It used to be legal for white people to own black people as property. It was legal for slave masters to beat or even kill their slaves. They could sell off a slave's wife or husband or even *children* if they wanted to. Did the fact that slavery was legal make it moral?"

The woman simply glared at me in silence.

"That's right," I continued. Long before the Supreme Court stupidly legalized abortion, it stupidly upheld the legality of slavery in its 1857 *Dred Scott* decision. Did that make it moral? Of course not. And what about the fact that it was completely legal in Germany during the Third Reich to round up Jews, forcibly relocate them into concentration camps, and then liquidate them in gas chambers? That was legal, but did that make it morally okay?"

At this, I could see the woman was about to explode with anger. A vein in her forehead was throbbing wildly. Before she could say anything, I blurted the next idea that popped into my head (which was nowhere near as heinous as those first two legal-but-still-immoral scenarios, but was the proverbial straw that broke the camel's back).

"And what about the fact that in the United States, prior to 1920, it was perfectly *legal* for men to prevent women from voting in elections. Was *that* okay simply because it was . . ."

At that, the woman stormed off. I have no idea if she eventually came back to pay for the stuff she was waiting in line to purchase, but this I do know: She clearly had felt she was on the moral high ground about abortion, being anti-large families, and whatever else she was up in arms about that day, but she was utterly unprepared for someone to poke holes in her "It wouldn't *be* legal if it weren't moral!" illogic. She was arguing from a moral-relativist position, which is one of the easiest fallacies to disprove. All you have to do, as I discovered, is simply turn the tables so that something the moral relativist holds dear is relativized, with predictable results.

I still think about that angry woman and wonder if she's come to that realization. She unwittingly taught me a lesson that day, which I've had countless opportunities to practice and refine as I've learned how to effectively turn those tables. There are many effective (and fun!) ways to do it. Two of my favorites:

She says: "Don't push your morality on me."

I say: "Wait. You mean, I don't have a right to my opinion?"

She says: "Yes, you have a right to your opinion, but you don't have a right to force your opinion on other people."

I say: "Oh really? Is that your opinion? So why are you trying to force *your* opinion on me?"

And:

He says: "There's no such thing as objective truth. So, you can't say that abortion is 'wrong.' It's just something you disagree with."

I say: "So, is it objectively true that there's no such thing as objective truth?"

He says: "Well, . . ."

"Behold, sons are a heritage from the Lord,
   the fruit of the womb a reward.
Like arrows in the hand of a warrior
   are the sons of one's youth.
Happy is the man who has
   his quiver full of them!
He shall not be put to shame
   when he speaks with his enemies in the gate"
(Ps 127:3–5).

Chapter 38

The Fight

I GOT into my first serious fistfight when I was in the fourth grade. I say serious because a bloody nose was involved, and it wasn't mine. A kid in my class—the supremely annoying *Daniel*—who sat in the desk directly behind me found endless ways to harass me. You know, things like blowing on my neck until I'd raise my hand to complain to the teacher, or flicking my ear lobe hard with his middle finger teeing off from his thumb, or shooting tiny spit wads of balled up paper into my hair, or targeting me with fourth-grade school yard name-calling during recess, and so forth. It was constant.

Daniel really, really irritated me—so much so, that even now, nearly fifty years later, I still remember his smirking freckled face. He devised a novel way to embarrass and antagonize me, which was to announce loudly to the other kids that my initials, P.M., actually stood for "Poop Manure." Good times.

The fistfight in question went down one afternoon as another kid and I were walking across a long field that separated my neighborhood from the school. I remember it in uncanny detail, even after all these years.

This kid's family had recently come over from Romania or Hungary or some other impoverished Eastern European country that languished behind the Iron Curtain. It was tough enough for the poor kid that he started school halfway through the academic year, which rendered him friendless at the start. But this was compounded by his shabby, odd, ill-fitting Eastern-European clothes and shoes and his halting English spoken with a weird Eastern-European accent, which cemented his status as a pariah.

And, as you might expect, Daniel zeroed in on him immediately, capitalizing on the boy's social awkwardness with relentless mockery. Which is why a fight was inevitable when Daniel and a few of his cronies intercepted us traipsing across the field after school. The last several months of anger and frustration began to boil up inside me as soon as I saw them approach.

Ignoring me, Daniel moved in close and started circling my awkward friend, taunting him, pushing him around, and jeering at his accent, clothes, etc. His cronies egged him on.

I shouted, "Cut it out, you stupid *jerk!*" just as Daniel shoved the kid to the ground, knocking his glasses into the dirt, kicking him in the side a couple of times as he writhed on the ground, crying. Then he rounded on me with a glare.

"Who are you calling *jerk?*" he barked, moving toward me menacingly. What happened next was a blur. As he stepped toward me, his fists raised, I lunged at him, propelled by a school year's worth of pent-up frustration and anger. My rage boiled up like lava from an emotional reservoir deep inside that I didn't even know existed until it suddenly overwhelmed me. Grabbing a fistful of Daniel's shirt with my left hand, I hit him square in the face as hard as I could with my right.

Though I was only a puny fourth-grader, I felt a sensation of power that I had never felt before as my fist cracked solidly against his face. That stupid smirk of his was gone, and a rush of satisfaction swept over me as Daniel stumbled backward, landing on his back. I then sat on his chest and pinned his arms to the ground with my knees and began to pummel his face with more punches, as hard as I could, until his friends pulled me off.

One of those punches had given him a bloody nose and another had opened a gash above his left eyebrow. He was crying and bleeding as he struggled to his feet. He backed away, shouting at me to leave him alone and stay away from him, and that he was going to tell his mom, and she was going to call the police on me, I was going be in big trouble, etc.

That fight ended my troubles with Daniel and, as I recall, he never troubled that foreign kid again either. I got lucky that day. I won that fight because I caught him by surprise, but it could easily have gone the other way. True, I learned a valuable lesson about how to handle bullies. Standing up to them doesn't always work, but it often does.

And yet, that's not the primary lesson I learned that afternoon. Yes, it's necessary and even righteous, at times, to stand up and defend the weak and defenseless, but we have to do so in a righteous way. Rage and a desire for revenge had overwhelmed me. *That's* why I won that fight. Daniel was just being his mean self. I was out for blood and retribution for all those times he had bothered or belittled me. It was that frightening new sensation of being totally carried away by anger—being nearly *out of control* with anger—that kind of scared me.

I was right to fight but wrong to seek revenge. It's good to defend someone weaker but bad to go beyond what's sufficient to settle the matter. Righteous indignation has its proper place but revenge and retribution never do.

Ever since, that fistfight and the memory of how quickly my anger engulfed me that day has remained an iconic reminder of the danger of letting base emotions overpower reason. It's how bad decisions are made, how crimes of passion happen, and how permanent, irretrievable damage can be done to marriages, friendships, careers, and even one's immortal soul.

"Be not quick to anger, for anger lodges in the bosom of fools" (Eccl 7:9).

"Be angry but do not sin; do not let the sun go down on your anger, and give no opportunity to the devil" (Eph 4:26–27).

"Know this, my beloved brethren. Let every man be quick to hear, slow to speak, slow to anger, for the anger of man does not work the righteousness of God" (Jas 1:19–20).

Chapter 39

The Absentminded Samaritan

IN THE parable of the Good Samaritan (*cf.* Lk 10:25–37), Jesus relates how, after highway robbers had accosted and beaten a man nearly to death, a virtuous stranger appears and saves him. Inconveniencing himself and spending his own money on food, lodging, and medical care for the victim, the Good Samaritan tells the innkeeper, "Take care of him; and whatever more you spend, I will repay you when I come back." Like most Christians, I learned this inspiring story in my childhood and, like most Christians, always considered myself cut from the same cloth as the Good Samaritan. *Of course* I would be like him and help a total stranger out, if ever I happened across a similar situation.

One particular incident stands out in my mind. I was in my car heading back to work from my lunch break when I spotted a motorist in need—an elderly woman, whose car must have conked out, was stranded on the shoulder of a busy thoroughfare. She beamed as I pulled up behind her and hopped out to see how I could help. I wondered how long she had been stuck there and how many inconsiderates had whizzed by her without bothering to help.

"Hello, ma'am." I smiled helpfully. "Car trouble?"

"Thank you for stopping to help, young man. Yes, something is wrong with it, but I have no idea what. Could you take a look at it?"

Although I've never been mechanically inclined, being a male and all, and her being a female (albeit older than my grandmother), I went through the obligatory motions of checking under the hood to see if there was "engine trouble." But I had no clue what to look for, so I wiggled a few wires and tugged on a few engine parts and asked her to try starting it again. No go. The gas gauge indicated that the tank wasn't empty. And with that, the full extent of my automotive expertise had been exhausted.

"Hmm. Looks like you'll have to have it towed to a garage," I said. "I'm not sure what's wrong with it." (My opinion on the condition of her car was about as worthless as my opinion on how to perform brain surgery or land a jet fighter on the deck of an aircraft carrier.) "I'd be happy to give you a lift into town, though, if you'd like."

"Thank you, no," she said. I could sense her wariness of riding off with a stranger, even one who was earnest and helpful. "But I would appreciate it if you would call my son and let him know I'm out here." She handed me a scrap of paper on which she had jotted her son's name and phone number, as well as her own name. "He lives in town, and he can come pick me up."

"I'm happy to help, ma'am," I assured her. "I'll call your son right away, as soon as I get to work and have him come get you. Shouldn't be more than ten minutes." I drove off with a wave and a smile. In the rearview mirror, I saw her smile and wave back. I felt good about myself, helping someone in need like that, especially such a kindly old lady. What a *Great* Samaritan I was!

That night after dinner, I remembered I had forgotten to call her son.

Argh! How long had that poor woman been stuck out there on the side of the road? For hours, no doubt. Had anyone else stopped to help, or was she, God forbid, still out there in the dark, waiting for her son to come find her—her son who had no clue where she was and that her car had broken down because I had totally forgotten to do what I promised? I felt terrible that I had let her down by being so stupidly forgetful and could just imagine her ire, an hour or two or three after she watched me drive off to fetch help, when she realized help wasn't coming, at least not because of me.

I debated whether to drive twenty minutes across town back to the spot where I'd found her, but decided against it because, surely, by now, someone would have stopped to help, right?

What a dufus! My scatterbrained, unthinking, perfunctory attempt at being a Good Samaritan almost certainly made that lady's already inconvenient situation a lot more aggravating. What did I learn from this? Well, first, that I need to follow through when I make a promise. When I say I'm going to do something—especially when someone else is really depending on it—I must do it. Yes, it's sometimes easier said than done, and I sometimes fail in this regard, but it's the ideal to strive for because good intentions are not enough. Happy talk and empty gestures don't do any good.

I learned another important lesson: Thinking about someone is not the same as praying for that person.[1] Saying, "I'll

---

[1] Prayer is a concentrated act of the intellect and the will, which often involves an intentional calling out to God from the heart with a petition. Other prayer forms involve repentance and sorrow for sin, as well as praising and adoring God.

pray for you," or "My thoughts and prayers are with you," if you don't follow through and actually *pray* for that person, can be just as empty and inconsequential as saying, "Sure, I'll call your son right away. No problemo. I got this. No worries. Done deal."

"God is not man, that he should lie, or a son of man, that he should repent. Has he said, and will he not do it? Or has he spoken, and will he not fulfil it?" (Nm 23:19).

"Not everyone who says to me, 'Lord, Lord,' shall enter the kingdom of heaven, but he who does the will of my Father who is in heaven" (Mt 7:21).

Chapter 40

My Hero

"**M**Y DAD can beat up your dad!" is taunt most little boys will at some point shout at a rival. This is because fathers are archetypes of masculinity. They image to their children—for better or for worse—what it means to be a man, dad, husband, protector, and provider. And children learn lessons from their fathers—for better or for worse—that remain indelibly imprinted for life. It happened thus to me.

As I survey the circuitous path of life I've traveled thus far, not always knowing where I was headed, though always aware of where I had started, it's clear that many of the decisions I made along the way, causes I came to espouse, attitudes I adopted, mistakes I made, and successes I met with, were all in some way or another the result of lessons I learned from my father, Bernard E. Madrid.

Born in El Paso in 1937, the third of six children, he grew up speaking only Spanish in a devoutly Catholic Mexican family whose members had been forced in the 1920s to flee their haciendas, factories, and government jobs in Mexico when the Revolutionary reign of anti-Catholic terror became overwhelming. My paternal grandmother, Esperanza, recounted stories about how desperately bad things had gotten in Mexico when she was young.

Once, Pancho Villa and his gang descended on her home in search of her father, a judge in the town of Camargo, 100 miles south of Chihuahua. Providentially, my great grandfather caught wind of the raid just in time to don some peasant clothes, clamber onto a burro, and hightail it out into the desert where he waited for Pancho Villa and his men to leave, after they had loitered for a couple of days intending (unsuccessfully) to shoot my grandfather when he returned. She told me thrilling stories of the heroic young Jesuit martyr, Fr. Miguel Pro, who carried out a clandestine priestly ministry in Mexico City, always wearing disguises, successfully eluding the authorities who frantically searched for him for two years before finally capturing and executing him by firing squad.

My dad heard those same true stories of heroic Catholicism as he grew up, and I believe they had the same effect on him that they did on me. He passed on to me an ardent love for the Catholic Faith, a deep knowledge of its teachings, and a keen awareness of the danger and suffering that sometimes occasion being a faithful Catholic in the midst of persecution.

Several of my earliest memories of my dad are from 1963, when I was three. Memories of him tossing me playfully into the air, catching me, as fathers do, and laughing loudly as I whooped and hollered with glee, a father-son duet of closeness. Memories of riding me around on his back in the small yard of our duplex in Monrovia. Those and all the other fun and funny moments I can recall of him from back then when he was a young man are a trove of colorful, if faded, postcards from my childhood.

One stark, early memory is of what happened on November 24 of that year, two days after President Kennedy was assassinated. I don't remember anything about the assassination itself, other than a few vague flashbacks of seeing my parents crying and distressed (I had never seen my dad cry) and another fleeting memory of being with them at church, praying with many other people who were also crying and distraught. What I do remember vividly, almost photographically, is sitting next to my dad on the couch in our living room and seeing a man get shot to death on live TV.

My dad and I and everyone else in the country who happened to be in front of the TV news at that moment watched in horrified disbelief as Lee Oswald, Kennedy's assassin, was gunned down by Jack Ruby while being led in handcuffs through the parking garage of the Dallas Police Department headquarters. I didn't understand what was happening and was startled when my dad leapt to his feet and started freaking out, shouting agitatedly.

As an adult, I asked him about that day, wondering what he remembered of it. He confirmed the details of my mental image of the event and described his shock and anger that the man who killed the president had taken his secrets to the grave.

Another memory I still see, like a photograph in my mind: I'm about three. Standing in the doorway of the bathroom in our modest home, I'm watching my dad shave. He's wearing a white tee shirt and slacks and is leaning toward the mirror, his face lathered in Burma Shave. Passing the razor across his face, he talks to me and I to him, though about what, I'm not sure. This visual echo from my past is suffused with the impression that my dad was telling me that someday I, too, would grow up to be a man and that I, too, would shave. That such a mundane and easily forgettable vignette—shaving—could become an iconic memory of that long-ago father-son moment fascinates and puzzles me. Why then, why that? It is the mystery of memories.

All I know is that this particular interaction with my dad, for some reason, made an indelible impression on me then, one that hasn't dimmed with the passage of time. It was a life lesson about life itself, how time passes and things change and how we're all heading toward a goal. Ultimately, that goal is God Himself. The profound mystery of the great *exitus-reditus* (leaving and returning) of life and being and of all God's creatures who come from Him and return to Him was ever so slightly unveiled before me that day I watched my father shave. His simple words about growing up were, as I reflect on them now, a faint tracing of the arc of being that reaches toward our final fulfillment in eternity.

There was something casually heroic and debonair about my father, especially as a young man. Remembering back to when he was in his mid-twenties, not long out of the military and at the peak of his physical perfection, his wavy, jet-black hair, broad smile of straight, white teeth, taut physique and bulging biceps made him seem like a coiled steel spring. And though I never saw it happen, I'm quite sure he *could* have gone mano a mano with any other dad and won. In this, my dad was a paradigm of manhood for me. A protector, provider, and leader.

Once, when I was eight, Mr. Morrison from across the street showed up at our home around midnight, drunk and belligerent, banging the front door and shouting nonsense. Rather than calling the cops and waiting for them to handle things, my dad bravely opened the door and confronted the 6' 3" 230-pound bruiser. Then he physically barred him from barging into our home. Wild eyed and gesticulating violently, the booze-addled man demanded, "Let me see your wife and kids!" and kept trying to push past my father but couldn't because he faced him down grappling with him until he had forced him off our porch and away from our house. Seeing he wasn't going to get past my dad, our psycho neighbor wandered off into the darkness shouting incoherencies. That lesson in bravery was very important to me.

I remember my dad spanked me a lot (or so it seems) when I was a kid, though that really says more about me than him. I was a mischievous kid and pretty much deserved every speaking I got—as well as those I didn't get because my parents weren't always wise to my shenanigans. I don't carry any grudges about getting spanked, grounded, and otherwise punished for my malfeasances growing up.

As life wore on and my dad began to shoulder more and more of the cares life riding herd on a big family can pile on (I'm the oldest of eight), I can remember being dimly aware of how sometimes complicated and pressurized his life had become. His job as an electronics engineer paid enough to make ends meet but not much more. We had a comfortable home, though we lived simply, and though I can't recall ever going hungry, we ate very basic, humble food because that was pretty much all we could afford on my dad's paycheck. No-frills dinners of Hamburger Helper were common, or a plate of beans and rice, and of course a cheap-and-easy meal of tostadas or bean burritos was very common at Casa Madrid, which was never a problem for me because I love Mexican food.

But the frugality my dad exercised in our family budget contained other important lessons beyond how to make the most out of a dollar. I will never forget the sense of shock and admiration I felt when I was in the seventh or eighth grade and my mom explained to me that the reason my dad's wingtip shoes he wore every day to work had a nickel-sized hole clear through each sole was because he preferred to wear worn out shoes so that there'd be enough money for her to buy us kids shoes.

My dad sacrificed for us, really and truly, though he never said anything about it. Many times, I can remember eating a hasty breakfast with my siblings before heading off to school and there being just enough milk in the fridge for us kids to have cereal. It never occurred to me, until my mother explained what was happening, that my dad often skipped breakfast before work, not because he wasn't hungry, but because there wasn't enough food for him *and* us to eat our morning meal. You see, it was the little things, the quiet and unspoken things, he did that made the biggest impression on me.

Looking back, I see many lessons in justice in my dad's firm hand when meting out punishments. I also remember the many second chances he'd grant me, even when I didn't deserve one. Those lessons about justice and mercy—not from what he said, but from what he did and didn't do— enabled me to pursue a similar course with my own children, trying to instill in them a deep sense of God's love for us as the foundation of both his love and mercy. As Jesus said, quoting Hosea 6:6, "Go and learn what this means, 'I desire mercy, and not sacrifice.' For I came not to call the righteous, but sinners" (Mt 9:13).

So many of the life lessons my dad taught me were unspoken. He showed me by his life. For example, I've never in my life heard him utter a swear word. Not when some maniac would cut him off in traffic. Not when someone spoke harshly to him, or when I'd disobey him, or when some misfortune popped up unexpectedly. Not even when he'd hit his thumb with a hammer while working in the garage would he ever use profanity.

Oh sure, of course my dad could get angry, even furious, with people and situations (not being perfect and needing God's grace to make up for our shortcomings was another important lesson he imparted to me by word and example), but he never swore or cursed. And the powerful thing, for me at least, is that I don't recall him ever sitting down and lecturing me on the importance of avoiding foul language. He just showed me by how he lived.

When I got into high school and found myself experimenting briefly with profanity (mainly because some of the other kids used it regularly and I wanted to fit in), I soon realized how lame it was to talk like that and quickly dropped it like the bad habit it could easily have become, were it not for my dad's good example. It was then, I can see now, that I developed a positive *horror* of blasphemy. Hearing others take God's name in vain was and still is to this day an occasion of sadness and revulsion for me. I owe that to my dad.

And I'm grateful for that lesson. Purity of speech may not be the most important thing in life, but it is important and carries with it an indication of the inner person. My dad taught me by example that a true gentleman doesn't debase himself and those around him with profanity. "And he called the people to him and said to them, 'Hear and understand: not what goes into the mouth defiles a man, but what comes out of the mouth, this defiles a man'" (Mt 15:10–11).

The English word "hero" derives from the Latin *hērōs*, often used to refer to the demigods of ancient Greece and Rome. In time it came to mean someone of extraordinary talent or character. And it is in this sense that my father has been my hero. He's not a perfect man, of course—only Jesus is—but in his human imperfections and limitations my father, over his long life with its ups and downs, tragedies and triumphs, and all the hidden little mundane details in between that make up a lifetime, nonetheless reflected to me the image of God the Father, who is the sum of all perfections.

I don't *idolize* my dad, which would be both myopic and futile for, as he taught me, idols obscure God from our view and separate us from him. Rather, my dad has been for me an *icon* of what it means to be a man, father, and husband. In his own imperfections and limitations, he showed me what it means for God's grace to build on my nature.

———————————◆———————————

"Show yourself in all respects a model of good deeds, and in your teaching show integrity, gravity, and sound speech that cannot be censured" (Ti 2:7–8).

Chapter 41

The Friends

EARLY IN our marriage, Nancy and I enjoyed meeting new people with whom we developed friendships, though we started to notice that most of them didn't last very long. It was weird because though we seemed to have plenty in common with most of the young couples our age whom we befriended—you know, same parish, similar interests, kids, etc.—it seemed that after a few months, maybe a year at the most, things would begin to peter out.

The invitations for dinner or backyard barbecues became less and less frequent as did the phone calls. It eventually dawned on us that unless *we* made the initiative to call or get together, nothing would happen. Was there something odd or off-putting about *us*, we wondered? Had we done something to offend? That was certainly possible, we figured, at least once in a while, here or there, but regularly? Come on.

Perplexed, Nancy and I even began to experiment to see how long it would take for the now familiar trend to play out again, how long it would take for a formerly warm and promising acquaintance with another couple to cool and evaporate. Consciously observing the process didn't make it any more comfortable for us, but we gradually became less puzzled. What we learned together, and what I have learned in my own way personally over many years is that what we initially mistook for *friendships* were really just friendly, comfortable acquaintanceships with congenial and attractive people with whom, for a time, we had enough in common to generate some fun times, a few laughs, and not a whole lot else.

We discovered that virtually none of these shiny happy people were actually our *friends*. Back then, neither we nor they really understood what true friendship is and why, though it's certainly pleasant to hang out with fun, interesting, like-minded people, true friends are actually pretty few and far between.

It is true, as C. S. Lewis famously said, that "friendship . . . is born at the moment when one man says to another 'What! You too? I thought that no one but myself . . .' "

Some of my own dearest, lifelong friendships sprang into existence on the occasion of similar realizations. Even so, as I came to see, a true and lasting friendship has something durable and resilient about it that enables the two friends to weather not just the storms of life but also the monotonies, geographical distance, hectic schedules, and the myriad mundane cares of life, all of which are quite capable of stifling a growing friendship with simple inertia or inattention.

That's what Nancy and I didn't understand about our friends early on. They were busy, we were busy, time marches on, and though the fun times were fun and all, fun isn't sufficiently deep soil for the roots of a true friendship to sink down, take root, and thrive. And once this simple truth began to come into view, hazily at first, I started learning the meaning of true friendship, which made it easier to recognize a real friend when I found one.

I've always loved this description: true friendship does not consist of two people standing face-to-face, gazing at each other, but two people standing side-by-side gazing in the same direction. What I learned was that *that* kind of friendship—everything from man and wife in holy matrimony, to members of a band of brothers, and every other type in between—enjoys permanence and stability when it is grounded in a common goal shared by the two. The more noble and beautiful the goal, the more noble and beautiful the friendship.

The Beatles' classic song "In My Life" offers a poignant, if secular, expression of this truth:

> There are places I remember
> All my life though some have changed
> Some forever not for better
> Some have gone and some remain
> All these places have their moments
> With lovers and friends I still can recall
> Some are dead and some are living
> In my life I've loved them all
> But of all these friends and lovers
> There is no one compares with you
> And these memories lose their meaning
> When I think of love as something new
> Though I know I'll never lose affection
> For people and things that went before
> I know I'll often stop and think about them
> In my life I love you more
> Though I know I'll never lose affection
> For people and things that went before
> I know I'll often stop and think about them
> In my life I love you more
> In my life I love you more

Now I can see clearly what was nearly invisible to me when I was young: True, good, lasting friendships are relatively rare. And that's good. It's fine to have many acquaintances with who you can share a laugh or a meal, but a true friend is a great treasure well worth waiting for. I'm thinking, with profound gratitude to the Lord, of those few lifelong friends of mine whom I treasure.

◆

"*There are friends who pretend to be friends,*
> *but there is a friend who sticks closer than a broth-*
> *er*" (Prv 18:24).

"*Greater love has no man than this, that a man lay down his life for his friends*" (Jn 15:13).

Chapter 42

The Sand Pebbles

THE SAYING, "some things cannot be unseen," is true—sometimes *painfully* true. It's a lesson I've had to learn and relearn countless times over the years, much to my regret as I look back on it.

The first time it happened, though, wasn't my fault. I was only about nine-years-old when one of my uncles, who's just seven years older than me, dragged me along to the local cinema to see *The Sand Pebbles*, starring Steve McQueen. Of course, I had no business seeing such a movie at that deeply impressionable age, but my sixteen-year old uncle lied to my parents about what he planned to see, so they let me tag along, unaware of his real intentions.

Almost as soon as the movie started, I began to feel anxious and afraid. I was traumatized by the brutal violence that assaulted me from the big screen—graphic depictions of appalling things I had never before imagined, much less seen—racism, horrifying accidents involving heavy machinery, gruesome torture, murder, and a particularly upsetting scene of a mercy killing. It was horrible. About halfway through, I couldn't take it anymore. Bolting from my chair, I ran out to the lobby crying, and there I stayed, alone in an inconspicuous corner, until the movie ended and my uncle sauntered out and started making fun of me for being a "baby" and not being tough enough to watch.

I don't remember whether I told my parents what happened when I got home, but I don't think I did. For a long time afterward I had nightmares about that movie. There was no way I could unsee what I had seen. Even today, if I close my eyes and cast my mind back to that day, I can still see those terrifying images. I wish I couldn't, but some things cannot be unseen.

I also wish I could tell you I learned my lesson that first time, early on, with *The Sand Pebbles*. If only I had. Alas, one of life's more painful lessons, at least for me, and I suspect for many, is that I so often assumed that certain things I freely chose to look at couldn't harm me. How wrong I was. But I thank God for his gift of grace that can purify our memories and soothe our imaginations when they have been clawed and lacerated by the hideous or forbidden things we might choose to gaze upon. It's like staring into the sun. If you're not careful, it can blind you.

"The eye is the lamp of the body. So, if your eye is sound, your whole body will be full of light; but if your eye is not sound, your whole body will be full of darkness. If then the light in you is darkness, how great is the darkness!" (Mt 6:22–23).

"Do not love the world or the things in the world. If anyone loves the world, love for the Father is not in him. For all that is in the world, the lust of the flesh and the lust of the eyes and the pride of life, is not of the Father

but is of the world. And the world passes away, and the lust of it; but he who does the will of God abides forever" (1 Jn 2:15–17).

Chapter 43

The Neighbor

IFIRST saw pornography when I was twelve. Boyishly innocent and utterly unprepared for the jarring, damaging
experience, I was too embarrassed and ashamed to mention
it to anyone, least of all my parents. I was also mesmerized
by it.

By today's standards, awash as we are in a highly eroticized
culture that seems more or less normal to many (especially
younger people), it may seem quaint to some that I was "that
old" before I encountered porn, which is sad. Sadder still is
the enormously deleterious impact pornography has had
on our culture since the 1950s, when its leprous tentacles
began to slither out of the confines of back alleys and seedy
bookstores in the "bad part of town" and into the mini-mar-
kets, theaters, hotels, and homes of America, much of which
intruded by way of that once cutting-edge new technology
known as the VHS cassette. "Be kind, please rewind" we
were told.

If only it were possible to rewind the culture back to before
the plague of porn had begun to take hold. How different our
society might have been. How different *we* might have been.
It's like wondering what the world would have been like if
only Adam and Eve had done the right thing and obeyed
God's minimal directive:

The LORD God took the man and put him in the garden of Eden to till it and keep it. And the LORD God commanded the man, saying, "You may freely eat of every tree of the garden; but of the tree of the knowledge of good and evil you shall not eat, for in the day that you eat of it you shall die." (Gn 2:15–17)

Something died in me that day I first went to our neighbor's house to feed his cats and fish and water the plants. A school teacher in his thirties, he seemed nice enough, kind of bohemian, with a beard, longish hair, and a casual jeans and tweed sports-jacket look. He and his wife and daughter were to be away on vacation for two weeks and, one day, when he spotted me watering our front lawn with the garden hose, he walked over and asked if I'd be available to look after their pets and plants while they were gone. "I'll pay you $25," he smiled.

That was far more money than I'd ever had at one time. Excited by the opportunity to get a little extra jingle in my pocket (a kid could buy a *lot* of bubble gum and baseball cards with that kind of cash), I ran inside and asked my dad breathlessly if it would be okay. Grinning, I rushed back out and informed our neighbor that I could do it. "Great!" he said, handing me a key to their front door. "Stop by tomorrow," he said, "and I'll show you where the cat food and everything is."

He didn't need to show me where everything was. Everything was quite easy to find, in fact, it was practically impossible *not* to find for an inquisitive twelve-year-old who, *with permission from an adult*, had the run of the house. They had pornographic magazines everywhere, hundreds of them, some strewn carelessly on coffee tables and upright in book cases, but mainly stored in boxes, big cardboard boxes filled to the brim with stacks of *Playboy* and *Penthouse*. I spent the next two weeks dutifully tending to my neighbors' cats and plants but also to my own newly inflamed curiosity about the awful, beguiling contents of those boxes.

Now, forty-five years later, how I wish I could somehow rewind back to that long ago day when my innocence was still intact and could well have remained so for years to come. Many people, maybe most, harbor sorrow for their lost innocence. Thankfully, as I also discovered, God's grace is more powerful than our sins, and his loving providence is more powerful than human corruption. It was around that same time that I began to discover the healing power of the Sacrament of Penance.

Sometimes I wondered what became of that wretched man, may God have mercy on him. And I've never been able to read the following Bible passage without thinking of him and ruing the day he approached me with his fateful question.

———————— ••• ———◆——— ••• ————————

"Whoever causes one of these little ones who believe in me to sin, it would be better for him if a great millstone were hung round his neck and he were thrown into the sea" (Mk 9:42).

"And he said to his disciples, 'Temptations to sin are sure to come; but woe to him by whom they come! It would be better for him if a millstone were hung round his neck and he were cast into the sea, than that he should cause one of these little ones to sin'" (Lk 17:1–2).

"Woe to the world for temptations to sin! For it is necessary that temptations come, but woe to the man by whom the temptation comes! And if your hand or your

foot causes you to sin, cut it off and throw it from you; it is better for you to enter life maimed or lame than with two hands or two feet to be thrown into the eternal fire" (Mt 18:7–8).

"No temptation has overtaken you that is not common to man. God is faithful, and he will not let you be tempted beyond your strength, but with the temptation will also provide the way of escape, that you may be able to endure it" (1 Cor 10:13).

Chapter 44

The Mansion

NANCY AND I bought our first house in early 1985, a few weeks after our third child, Timothy, was born. We figured it would be a decent place for our small but growing family, at least for a few years, till we could save enough to get into a more spacious home. At least, that was our plan at the time. And you know the old saying, "If you want to make God laugh, tell him your plans."

Our house was small—1,165 square feet, to be exact—two bedrooms and 1.5 baths, a tiny kitchen, a breakfast nook and dining room, a cozy living room, and that's it. But coming from our even smaller apartment, the new house (*our* new house) seemed roomy by comparison. That first week, as we were still emptying boxes and settling in, Nancy remarked happily and in all sincerity how *nice* it was that there were some rooms she didn't even have to go into on any given day—that's how luxuriously capacious our new digs seemed then. To us, it was a mansion.

With a few creative do-it-yourself jigs and pokes we turned the dining room into a third bedroom once our fourth child, Hillary, came along. We had only one car at the time, so when I was at work Nancy walked the kids back and forth to the local parish grammar school they attended, three blocks away. Getting to the grocery store and other errands was a little trickier for her with all the kids, so that was a Saturday event most weeks. Perhaps our neighbors, who noticed us traipsing to and from Mass each Sunday morning, smiled, or marveled, or tsk-tisked with disapproval as we passed by pushing a stroller, toddlers in tow, and mama out to here with each new baby on the way.

The years passed, the babies kept coming, and we were happy; a bit crowded, yes, but very happy. Our life then was so much simpler, and even though with didn't have much, we had a great time. Not exactly *poor*, but definitely financially tight all the time. As with many young families struggling to make it, we usually had more month left at the end of the paycheck, and money was carefully parceled out, though our bill-juggling not infrequently meant we had to decide which bill to pay late most months. But we also learned it's true that income rises to meet expenses!

One lesson I learned over and over again is how God will not be outdone in generosity. He really won't, as Nancy and I can testify. Our little "yes" to his plan for our marriage— eleven children, in our case—has been tiny compared to his largesse in all the ways that really matter. The Lord blessed us with so much life it was impossible not to be buoyed up and carried along by all the love that flowed from that blessing. Our little mansion was where the truth of God's promises became real and abiding:

"Give," he promises, "and it will be given to you; good measure, pressed down, shaken together, running over, will be put into your lap. For the measure you give will be the measure you get back" (Lk 6:38). God always provides. Always. This is one lesson I delight in sharing whenever possible with younger couples who sometimes wonder if they can *handle* all the blessings God might send them!

Eventually, we outgrew our mansion. By the summer of 1994, we had seven children stacked like firewood in those 1,165 square feet, and it was definitely time to move. (The fact that baby eight was on the way was an unmistakable clue).

More than anything, what I remember of those early years was how much fun and joy and music and laughter and mirth there was within the walls of our humble home. Life wasn't perfect, but whose life is? Like all couples, Nancy and I had our share of problems, burdens, and challenges, including a few that were serious, but even so, when difficult times arose, we found they were always surmountable. We always made it through. I am so grateful for that season of simplicity and smallness. I learned so much from it, especially this:

> "If God so clothes the grass of the field, which today is alive and tomorrow is thrown into the oven, will he not much more clothe you, O you of little faith? Therefore do not be anxious, saying, 'What shall we eat?' or 'What shall we drink?' or 'What shall we wear?' [or 'Where will we put all these *kids*?!']. For the Gentiles seek all these things; and your heavenly Father knows that you need them all. But seek first his kingdom and his righteousness, and all these things shall be yours as well.
>
> "Therefore do not be anxious about tomorrow, for tomorrow will be anxious for itself. Let the day's own trouble be sufficient for the day." (Mt 6:30–34)

* * *

> *"Blessed are the poor in spirit, for theirs is the kingdom of heaven"* (Mt 5:3).
>
> *"The point is this: he who sows sparingly will also reap sparingly, and he who sows bountifully will also reap bountifully. Each one must do as he has made up his*

mind, not reluctantly or under compulsion, for God loves a cheerful giver. And God is able to provide you with every blessing in abundance, so that you may always have enough of everything and may provide in abundance for every good work. As it is written,
　'He scatters abroad, he gives to the poor;
　his righteousness endures forever.'
He who supplies seed to the sower and bread for food will supply and multiply your resources and increase the harvest of your righteousness" (2 Cor 9:6–10).

"God will supply every need of yours according to his riches in glory in Christ Jesus" (Phil 4:19).

Chapter 45

The Window Seat

ABOUT TWENTY years ago, en route to Austin to speak at a conference, I boarded my connecting flight at DFW airport. Passing through the first class cabin toward economy class, I was pleasantly surprised to see Governor George W. Bush seated in first class on the aisle, smiling and shaking hands with those who passed by and greeted him. Figuring he'd probably appreciate one less person making a fuss over him, I simply looked him the eye, smiled, and nodded a hello. He did the same as I as passed by. Cool, I thought. Another famous-person encounter story I can share with family and friends, not realizing that I was moments from a much different encounter that would teach me an important life lesson.

Being high up the American Airlines' frequent flyer food chain enabled me to board immediately after the first-class passengers, which meant economy class in the huge DC-10 aircraft was virtually empty when I stepped into it. The seating configuration (an important detail, as you'll see in a moment) was an aisle and window seat on each side of the plane and five seats in the center. I immediately noticed a very fat man sitting in 12-B, the outside aisle seat. The window seat next to him, 12-A, was barely visible, that's how big he was. He must have been 400 pounds—no exaggeration.

"Ha, ha," I chuckled and murmured something snarky under my breath about pitying "the poor person who has to sit next to *that* guy!" Still chuckling, I continued walking and glanced down at my boarding pass, noting that I had been assigned a nice window seat that happened to be . . . 12-A.

Suddenly, I was no longer chuckling. My head snapped up. I locked a gimlet eye on 12-A and just as I was about to hang a U-turn and ask a nearby flight attendant if I could be assigned to a different seat, a different flight attendant announced on the intercom that the flight was oversold and would be very full, so could everyone please place smaller bags on the floor beneath the seat in front of them, etc.

There was no way to turn around anyway, as the throng of passengers behind me was pressing ahead, forcing me inexorably toward the huge man in the aisle seat. There was simply no way I was getting a different seat. And I had to be in Austin for my lecture in a few hours, so a later flight was out of the question. I had no choice. I was stuck.

"Uh, excuse me," I muttered to the guy, glancing nervously at 12-A and wondering how I'd fit.

"Oh!" he exclaimed, looking up at me, in what was simultaneously an admission of embarrassment, a sheepish apology, and a good-natured greeting rolled into a single syllable. "Oh, I'm very sorry about the tight squeeze, sir . . ." he said as he labored mightily to extricate himself from 12-B.

I was embarrassed and uncomfortable and, to be honest, pretty ticked off that I had drawn the unlucky short straw and had to sit next to him. The flow of passengers behind me halted for a good minute or so as he struggled to get to his feet so I could slip past into my spot. It was then that I realized how embarrassed this poor man was—all eyes were on him as he let me by. Huffing and puffing, he apologized again, red-faced, in part, I'm sure to the exertion but also I think due to shame. He was incredibly polite and apologetic. "I'm very sorry about the armrest, sir, but . . ." he trailed off for a moment. "But as you can see, I'm just not able to put it down."

"No problem," I said gamely. "We'll manage." I felt bad for him, and I felt bad for me.

"I'm really sorry about this," he said. "I was hoping I'd get lucky and there'd be an empty seat next to me." Then he sank back into his chair, and that's when I really started to feel uncomfortable. Claustrophobic. He simply could not fit into his seat. He was far too big. The entire right side of my body, from knee to shoulder, was completely pressed into and surrounded by his warm corpulence.

The only word I can think of to describe it is *formfitting*. The man overflowed from his seat onto me. The left side of my face was pressed into the wall of the plane. There was nothing I could do but try to keep it together. I couldn't even ask the flight attendant for a ginger ale when she passed by with the drink cart because there was no room to lower my tray table, and even if I could have done so, I wouldn't have been able to raise my arm to drink it.

Mercifully, the flight only lasted about an hour, but in that hour, I learned a very important lesson about myself.

When I boarded the flight, the fat man was a joke to me, an object of derision. It was a joke to me that someone would have to suffer with that kind of obesity. It was a joke to me that someone would have to sit next to him—that is, until *I* was the guy who had to sit next to him. Then it became real, and I started thinking about the misery and embarrassment and probably loneliness this man had to live with every day.

I gained an appreciation during that very uncomfortable hour about the cross that some people have to bear of being morbidly obese, a reality I had honestly never bothered to wonder about, much less feel compassion for before then. I began to reflect on how difficult life must be for that man and others in his situation—the ridicule, the disapproving looks, people making condescending and cutting remarks under their breath (*like I did*, stupid me), the daily inconveniences, the physical difficulties, etc.

"My gosh," I asked myself as I sat there miserably, "how do people in this man's situation get through life?" There was no way I was going to ask such a question of him, he was already very embarrassed as it was. But I too was embarrassed because I had been so uncharitable and un-Christlike in my thoughts about him. People in that predicament are easy to make fun of, and it pained me to realize it.

Yes, I saw a future president on that flight, but much more importantly, I saw, or rather, the Lord revealed to me, an unpleasant side of myself that I didn't even realize was there. And I'm so glad he did.

"Finally, all of you, be of one mind, sympathetic, loving toward one another, compassionate, humble" (1 Pet 3:8, NABRE).

Chapter 46

The Mormon

ONE EVENING, at the conclusion of a parish lecture I gave on the history of the Catholic Faith, a Mormon gentleman in attendance asked if we could discuss further a few issues I had raised. "Sure thing," I said. As we walked over to the church hall where refreshments were being served, he asked me, "What was that curtsy thing you did up at the front of the church when your talk was over?"

I understood what he meant. "Oh, you mean when I dropped down for a moment on one knee? We call that a 'genuflection' in the Catholic Church, and we do that to show reverence for Jesus in the Blessed Sacrament." He nodded thoughtfully, his right hand holding his chin, as I explained the Real Presence and how the Blessed Sacrament is reposed in the metal tabernacle in the center of the sanctuary. I was pleased by his interest and the opportunity to teach him something central about the Catholic Church. My satisfaction subsided quickly, though, when a look of doubt passed over his face like a shadow obscuring the sun. He clearly wasn't buying what I had just told him.

"That's interesting," he said thoughtfully. "I guess I *have* heard before that Catholics believe all that, but I never really knew why. We Mormons don't regard the communion bread we use at our sacrament meeting as anything more than a symbol. An important symbol, of course, but just a symbol. It's just bread." He paused for a few moments and, just as I was about to continue my mini-lesson on the Real Presence, he interjected: "But I really don't get the impression that most Catholics believe what you just said about 'the Eucharist.'"

"*Oh?*" I asked, eyebrows arched. "You don't think so? And why is that?" His comment took be aback. I mean, as a Catholic I figured that I'd know a whole heck of a lot better than what he, a Mormon, could possibly know about what Catholics believe, especially on something as central and foundational to Catholicism as the Eucharist.

"Well," he said, "not to be disrespectful to you or anything, but I've been to several Catholic weddings where Mass was performed," (I decided not to interrupt and explain that the Mass isn't *performed*, it's *celebrated*) "and I've also been to Mass for other Catholic events, and the Catholics *I've* seen there sure didn't seem as though they believed what you just said about Jesus being in the Eucharist."

"What do you mean?" I queried.

"For example," he said, "I've seen Catholics going forward to get Communion chewing gum" (I decided not to interrupt to explain that we don't *get* Communion, we *receive* Communion). "Some Catholics look pretty bored. I've seen some waving to others as they go forward. In fact, I've watched to see if there's any 'before and after' difference in the attitudes or appearance of the Catholics I've seen take Communion. And there isn't, at least not that I've ever seen. They look disinterested and indifferent."

At this, I started feeling a bit uncomfortable because I knew what he was saying is true of some, maybe many, Catholics who *don't* show much if any reverence when receiving Holy Communion. I winced interiorly at a memory that flashed through my mind just then of an elderly woman organist at a Mass I attended years earlier who *didn't even stop playing* when the priest walked over to give her Communion. She kept playing with her right hand and, without looking away from the keyboard, she jerked out her arm and the priest palmed a host into her left hand. She popped it into her mouth as casually as if it had been a potato chip or a handful of popcorn.

That's when I realized, to my horror, that what this Mormon was describing—the generalized lack of respect for the Real Presence of Jesus in the Blessed Sacrament that stems directly from the generalized lack of *faith* that he is truly present—was actually true.

"As I say," he added. "I'm not trying to be disrespectful or anything, but I just don't think Catholics believe what you believe on this issue."

I stood there silently, letting the awful truth of his words sink in. How very tragic, I thought to myself, that Catholics could be so cavalier and careless that they literally *couldn't care less* about the single greatest gift Jesus gave to his Church in the Holy Eucharist. What the Mormon guy said next was the worst part.

"You see, if *I* believed what you believe about the 'communion bread,' I mean, if I truly believed that that is really *God himself* and not just a symbol, I would fall flat on my face and be prostrate before it—him. I would be so overcome with awe and worship. And I've never seen any Catholic show that kind of respect. So . . . I guess they just don't believe it."

I don't remember anything else of the conversation that evening. This Mormon had spoken a terrible truth so clearly and with such devastating accuracy that it's all I could think about for the rest our discussion. I've thought about it many times since.

And this is the lesson I learned from him: yes, we Catholics can edify and educate and evangelize non-Catholics when we try to, but we can also *dis*-edify, discombobulate, and *de*-evangelize them without even trying, without saying a word, simply by dint of our sheer laziness and complacency and our lack of reverence for sacred things.

———————————◆———————————

"Let us offer to God acceptable worship, with reverence and awe" (Heb 12:28).

Chapter 47

The License

THE FAMOUS line, "It was the best of times, it was the worst of times," rather aptly describes aspects of my life around the time I became legal to drive a car. For one thing, my dad made getting an A in chemistry a *sine qua non* requirement for getting my driver's license. And that was a huge drag.

"It's non-negotiable," he informed me. "Not a B, not a B+, not an A-. You get an A, and you can get your license. No A, no license." My dad was shrewd. Knowing my distaste for math and science, which was clearly reflected in the Cs and Ds I routinely got in those subjects, he knew that by tying the one thing I wanted most in the world (my license) to the one thing I wanted least (buckling down academically) he'd get the desired result. And he did.

That formerly "immovable object" gave way to the "irresistible force" of my wanting to drive. Yes, it was a pain, and I definitely didn't enjoy having to study hard and labor to learn chemistry and get As on my exams, but I did it because I wanted to get my license more intensely than I didn't want to study.

The day after I showed my dad my report card on which a big fat "A" had been duly entered next to "Chemistry," I went to the DMV, passed my tests, and became street legal. No pain, no gain, right?

Fast-forward maybe two weeks. I was joyriding with a buddy whose wealthy parents had given him a sharp VW bug for his sixteenth birthday (and, of course, *he* didn't have to get good grades for that). They gave him practically anything he wanted. That's probably why he was so cavalier about letting me drive his car. "Sure, go for it," he said without hesitating, as soon as I asked.

It was one of those perfect Southern California days—clear, azure blue sky, sunny and seventy-five degrees, lots of open road and, best of all, there was in my wallet a rectangular piece of laminated paper emblazoned with CALIFORNIA DRIVER LICENSE across the top.

So there I am, the wind in my hair, my elbow hanging jauntily out the window, a grin on my face, and Boston's "More than a Feeling" blasting on the 8-track player as I cruised down the 405 Freeway thinking, *this is as good as it gets!* Just then, with not a care in the world, I glanced up at the bug's rearview mirror and saw the flashing red lights of death. A California Highway Patrol cruiser was bearing down on me. Apparently he'd been there for a while because in the mirror I saw the officer vigorously jerking his thumb sideways in a *pull over NOW* motion.

Panic ensued.

As he wrote me a ticket, the patrolman informed me that I had been speeding fifteen miles per hour over the posted speed limit. He further informed me that this moving violation incurred not just a hefty fine but also the requirement that I appear in court so that a judge could "have speakings" with me about my reckless driving.

"One of your parents must accompany you to court," he added as he handed me the citation, "because you're a minor.

And don't miss the court date or there'll be a warrant issued for your arrest, and you really don't want that to happen." Yeah, right. He had no earthly idea how badly I really didn't want that to happen.

After giving me instructions on how to pull back on the roadway safely, "Have a nice day!" was the last thing he said before walking back to his cruiser.

This is where things got a bit interesting. You see, that same friend who was letting me drive his car was also having a big party at his house the following night. I had to attend, of course, in part because the garage band I played bass with was planning to set up and jam. And girls really like that kind of thing, you know, so I was highly incentivized to be there. And the really great thing was that his parents would be out of town for the weekend. Even better, his parents (who were truly insane for doing so), had stocked the fridge with beer and soft drinks, loaded up on popcorn, chips, and pretzels, and even gave him a hundred bucks for pizza delivery. I kid you not.

"They told me we could have beer, as long as no one who drinks any drives home," my friend explained nonchalantly.

"*What?*" I responded incredulously. "You can't be serious!" It was inconceivable that my mom and dad would ever do anything like that, but apparently his parents partied pretty hard themselves and didn't see anything wrong with letting their son go and do likewise.

"No, it's totally cool with my folks," he said, "just as long as we don't trash the house and, of course, we have to drink 'responsibly,' he added with a wink and a smirk."

I had already gotten permission from *my* folks not just to attend the party (they had no clue there would be beer there) but to spend the night and hang out with my buddy the next day, so I conveniently forgot to mention the speeding ticket when I got home later that day.

The party was about as raucous and rowdy as you might expect. The following day, after tidying up the house a bit, I hung out with my friend till late afternoon and then he drove me home. The next day was Sunday, and of course I didn't want to disturb my parents' Day of Rest with anything as inconvenient and bothersome as the news that their punk son, who had just gotten his driver's license, had also just gotten a speeding ticket. So, I decided just to let things ride. The following day, though, I had to reveal what happened because I had to report to court soon, and *one of my parents had to go with me.* And that's when things started to slide.

My dad was predictably angry, but in that it's-been-a-long-day-and-I'm-tired anger that, I knew from experience, would flare and then die down quickly, which is what I was banking on. You know. I'd get a stern talking to and warning not to let it happen again, and then I'd skate. And I came *this* close to that actually happening, until my mom intervened.

"Wait a minute," she said as she scrutinized the ticket. "Today's Monday. It says here you got this ticket on Thursday, right?" she looked up at me with an arched eyebrow.

"Uh, well, yes. That's right. I got the ticket on Thursday."

"And you went to that party on Friday, right? And then you stayed at your friend's house most of Saturday, *right*?"

"Uh . . . ."

"Which means you intentionally concealed this ticket from your father and me *before* the party. Right?"

And that's where things stopped sliding and completely fell apart. My parents were really ticked off about the ticket, but even more so about my hiding it from them so I could go to the party. They grounded me for a week and piled on a bunch of extra chores. And though the judge didn't restrict my driving privileges (I did, however, have to spend an entire Saturday at a remedial driving school in exchange for my ticket being expunged from my record), my parents surely did.

Eventually, when I was allowed to drive again, I had learned a few lessons. First, don't drive faster than the speed limit. Second, always keep an eye on the rearview mirror, just in case a highway patrolman's back there somewhere looking for his next "appointment." Third, don't conceal serious stuff from your parents. But the fourth and most important lesson of all is this: Getting your driver's license is an analogy for human freedom. It confers rights and privileges, yes, but also imposes certain limits, liabilities, and obligations. Getting behind the wheel of a car and heading out on the open road isn't simply a matter of going where you will as fast as you want. Nor is life.

The rules of the road (drive the speed limit, stay in your lane, use your blinker when making turns, don't drive on the sidewalk, give pedestrians the right of way, stop at red lights, etc.) are there for a very important purpose. When a motorist disregards and disobeys those rules, accidents happen, property gets smashed, injuries are inflicted, and sometimes people die. This is true of life. Real freedom doesn't consist in doing whatever you want, however you want, with whomever you want, just because you want to— that's *license*, not freedom).

I discovered that God's "rules and regs," his moral precepts, are designed to enable us to be truly free so we can become truly happy. That, by far, was the most important lesson I learned from the speeding ticket. I never again want to see those flashing red lights in the rearview mirror, either literally or figuratively.

———————————————◆———————————————

"The law of the LORD is perfect,
reviving the soul" (Ps 19:7).

Chapter 48

The Heart of the Home

THE BLESSED Virgin Mary is a central figure in the gospel accounts of the life of Jesus, though her recorded words are but few. "May it be done to me according to your word" (Lk 1:38, NABRE) she responds humbly to the angel who announced the Good News of Christ's Incarnation to her who, blessed among women, was chosen by God to be the mother of the Savior. This is the highest possible honor any human person could ever receive from the Lord! And yet, Mary's quiet, trusting response shows the depth of her humility.

"They have no wine" (Jn 2:3), she says softly to her son Jesus, with whom she was a guest at the Wedding at Cana. She trusted that he would do the right and necessary thing for the young couple and didn't seek to control or dictate what should happen. She simply advises the waiters, "Do whatever he tells you" (Jn 2:5).

I see in my own mother, Gretchen Jane Madrid, an exemplar of many of the Blessed Virgin Mary's virtues. Growing up, of course, I wasn't consciously aware of that fact, but as I look back on my childhood and adolescence—the time of life when one's mom has the greatest influence and impact—I can see how she was the heart of our home in ways that remind me of Mary in the Gospels.

A lifelong Catholic, my mom's lineage is mainly Irish on her father's side and Swedish on her mother's. She was born in Denver in 1940, but her family soon moved to Southern California and settled in the newly suburban community of Norwalk, just one street over from the house where my dad (who was just another neighborhood kid to her, at that time) lived with his family. As the story is told, he showed up on her doorstep one afternoon when she was fourteen or fifteen and asked her to the high school sock hop.

On October 25, 1958, two days after she turned eighteen, my mom and dad were married at St. Pius X parish in Santa Fe Springs. I came along two years later, the oldest of their eventual eight children, not counting two difficult miscarriages—one before me and one after, before my younger sister Lisa was born. After the complications resulting from her first miscarriage, the doctor informed my mom that she'd never have children.

But being a woman of deep faith and trust in God, she prayed with my dad for a miracle. And though "miracle" isn't *typically* the word that springs to mind for most people who know me, my parents rejoiced when I was born and attributed my birth at least in part to the intercession of St. Jude Thaddeus (the patron saint of impossible cases) whose help in conceiving a child they had invoked continuously, along with their prayers to the Lord. That's how I got the middle name Thaddeus, by the way. And I have no doubt that my mom must have laughed (and cried) over the irony of impossible cases being involved. Let's just say, I was a mischievous kid.

My mom was quite beautiful. She still is, of course, in the way that women who age gracefully are, but in her younger days, she was definitely a head-turner. Pictures of her and my dad in the early years of their marriage show a slim, vivacious, woman with luxurious, long, dark hair, pleasingly large eyes, and a lovely smile. I remember her lilting laugh. And my mom didn't just embody beauty, she conferred it on her surroundings.

Take our home, for instance. Even though she often had only a modest budget to work with, she made sure our home was always comfortable, bright, clean, and orderly. She decorated with good taste and aesthetic refinement. My childhood memories are imbued with a happy contentment largely due to her civilizing, beautifying supervision of our home.

My mom worked hard and ran a tight ship, always leading us kids by example when it came to doing chores and keeping the many moving parts of our busy family running smoothly.

My mom epitomized the diligent, industrious, competent, prudent, housewife of legend. You know, the June Cleavers, Margaret Andersons, and Harriett Nelsons of old-school television sitcom fame. Those were the moms whose kids came home from school to find them baking cookies and wearing a dress, high heels, and a string of pearls. No, my mom didn't dress like that around the house, but she was always there when we came home from school and always had something tasty as a snack.

These lessons I put to good use when I went in search of (and found) a great woman to marry and raise our children. Talk about a *life* lesson! If my own mother hadn't been such a good example to us kids of what loving, caring, dutiful motherhood is, we would have been ill-equipped in many ways for life.

My mom was thrifty, though not to a fault. She knew how to make the family food budget stretch, but man could she turn simple fare into a tasty meal. From her example, I learned lessons on moderation and frugality, which is not to say I always excelled in those virtues, but I did *learn* them from her and, as I got older and wiser, they've served me well as a husband and father.

My mom was nobody's fool. She could be quite shrewd and had keen insights into human nature, especially of the kid variety. One funny story about this stands out in my mind. Once in the early 1970s, my mom took me and my three younger siblings with her to a large S&H Green Stamps redemption center about thirty miles from our home one weekday morning when we were off school. For months she had saved up Green Stamps (she also saved Blue Chip Stamps), painstakingly pasting them by denomination in the redemption booklets (if you have no clue what I'm talking about, you're probably under forty-five years of age) and perusing the catalogs for household appliances and other items she really wanted but didn't have the discretionary income to afford.

So, after about an hour or so at the Green Stamps place redeeming the booklets and getting the things she'd had her eye on, we went back outside to our station wagon, only to find that she had locked her keys in the car. There they were, dangling from the ignition, tantalizing us, but there was no way to get to them short of breaking a window, and there was no way *that* was going to happen if you knew my dad. So, a little panicky, my mom said to us kids, "You stay right here. Don't move! I'll be right back in a minute. Pat, you're in charge till I get back."

She went inside to use the phone and called my dad, who was at work. This did not make him at all happy. In fact, when my mom came back out and found us standing right where she left us, I could tell from the look on her face that my dad probably got pretty steamed when she explained that she was stranded with the kids a good twenty miles away from his office and that the only way for him to unstrand her would be to take time off work, drive over here, and unlock the car with his set of keys.

"When your father gets here," she said with that look in her eye that meant *pay attention—I really mean it*, "I want you to be quiet. He's kind of mad about this interruption, so just be good and stay quiet."

So, as we loitered there, waiting for my irritated father to show up. I walked around the car a few times just killing time and looking at random stuff. I tugged on one of the locked door handles and found that, hey, it wasn't locked. "Hey, mom!" I shouted with a grin. "Look! This door isn't locked! I can get the keys out for you!" I figured I'd get a reward of some kind, or at least a little praise for being clever and helpful, but what my mom did next astonished me.

Tight-lipped and unhesitating, she reached over, locked the car door and closed it firmly, leaving the keys dangling where they were. "Do *not* tell your father that the car door was unlocked," she warned us sternly, "or you'll be in BIG trouble." She knew that if he found out he made the trip for nothing then he'd be ticked off. Needless to say, we didn't say a word about it to him when he showed up. In fact, I remember telling him *the rest of the story*, much to his amusement, maybe twenty years later, when we all had a good laugh over it. Bottom line: my mom was astute.

My mom was also diligent about teaching us the Catholic Faith from the time we were small. It would have been unthinkable for her and my dad to not take us to Sunday Mass, no matter how small or squirmy we once were. They were firm and decisive when it came to behaving at Church. If one of us kids was noisy, disruptive, or inattentive at Mass, let's just say they had ways of correcting such malfeasance to bring about the desired behavior. I learned from them, my mom in particular, how to train my own kids how to comport themselves at Mass.

Nowadays, it's rare to find a family whose kids grew up in the 60s and 70s, as I did, in which all the sons and daughters remained Catholic. But that's what happened with us—thank you, Lord, and thank you, mom and dad. Not a single one of us ever abandoned the Catholic Church, even after all these years. That's a miracle in itself, if you ask me.

My mom and dad taught us from an early age that our Catholic Faith wasn't merely something we did for an hour a week on Sunday. It wasn't just a club we belonged to or a kind of hobby that was fun to indulge in now and then. Our Catholic Faith, they taught us, is, or at least should be our identity—who we *are*, not merely what we do. Our parents were surely pious, though not weirdly so. Our house didn't smell of incense or have religious statues in every room, although we did have a large crucifix prominently displayed in our living room so that anyone who entered our home knew immediately that we were Catholic. Other images of Jesus and Mary were present as well, but always in a balanced and natural way that encouraged piety in us kids without turning the house into a religious museum or something like that.

It fell largely to my mom to ensure that I properly prepared for and duly received the sacraments. She taught me about Jesus's Real Presence in the Blessed Sacrament and the healing and strengthening power of the Sacrament of Reconciliation. All those many times she brought us kids with her to Adoration and Benediction paid big spiritual dividends as we grew up and went out on our own. No question about it. I didn't realize it then, but I sure do now. Thank you, mom.

My mom taught me how to pray. She introduced me to the Triune God, Father, Son, and Holy Ghost, from my earliest years, teaching me about Jesus as my Lord and Savior. She taught me about my guardian angel and how to invoke his special intercession with that simple, beautiful prayer I learned from her lips as I sat on her lap as a little boy:

> Angel of God, my guardian dear, to whom God's love entrusts me here. Ever this day, be at my side to light, to guard, to rule, and guide, amen.

My mother not only taught me about the Blessed Virgin Mary and her tender maternal care for me, she exemplified that love—sometimes tough love, when I made it necessary— in how she prayed with me and for me. I have no doubt my mom has spent countless hours in prayer for her children, starting with me. And Lord knows there have been times in my life, perhaps most especially when she wasn't even aware of things I was dealing with and going through, that my mom's prayers helped carry me through. I came to better understand the truth and beauty and importance of the Blessed Virgin Mary's role in God's plan of salvation because I experienced the truth and beauty and importance of my mom's role in God's plan for my own family. She was always the heart of our home.

One special lesson my mom taught me as I grew up was to be close to Our Lady, especially by praying the Rosary. We prayed the Rosary many evenings together as a family. I often found it boring, though not always, and in later years, when I hit turbulence and difficulties in life, often of my own making, I found myself falling back, again and again, to praying the Rosary for guidance and help. The Rosary, for me, was sometimes a weapon against pernicious sin in my life, sometimes a key to unlock and swing wide seemingly impenetrable doors, sometimes a consolation when I felt lonely or confused, or an anchor when the storms of life swept over me and I needed grounding and stability. I'm deeply grateful to my mom for teaching me to pray the Rosary and love Mary, my heavenly mom.

There are so many other lessons, large and small, I learned from my mom's example and her admonitions, but a final one stands out that made a big impression on me: her and my dad's heroic generosity with God and with others. I remember countless times that they opened our home to people in need, to men and women and sometimes families who needed a meal or a place to stay.

In the aftermath of the fall of Saigon in 1975 and the subsequent influx of Vietnamese refugees into the United States, my parents volunteered to help at the refugee center at Camp Pendleton Marine Corps Base. For months, they gave up many of their Saturdays to drive down to the camp and spend hours volunteering. They also welcomed into our home a Vietnamese family of three adult siblings (two sisters in their early twenties and their eighteen-year-old brother). They lived with us for a year until they were able to get on their feet and move into their own place. It was a truly marvelous experience, and the Vietnamese food we feasted on that year was out of this world.

The most significant lesson in generosity, however, happened when I was about twenty and already on my own. My parents heard from someone at their parish that a South Korean orphan boy was in desperate need of an adoptive family in the United States. He had a serious heart problem that could be corrected surgically, though the operation wasn't available in Seoul, where he was living. If an American family would adopt the two-year old child, he would be able to come to the U.S. and have the operation.

My mom and dad didn't even hesitate before volunteering. Keep in mind, they already had their hands full with eight children of their own (one of whom had already died in infancy). But they said yes. Within a few months, Eugene (named after my mom's father) made the trip from Korea and had the operation at a hospital in Southern California. His heart problem was successfully corrected, but, tragically, enough time had passed due to red tape that the lack of oxygen to this little boy's brain caused by the heart abnormality resulted in the onset of cerebral palsy. Eugene had become severely mentally retarded and unable to care for himself.

My parents didn't blink an eye. Eugene was a member of our family from day one. And because my dad was gone at work all day, it fell to my mom to care for Eugene in every way, changing his diapers, bathing him, feeding him, and teaching him, just as she did all the rest of us when we were little. But in Eugene's case, she did so, without ever complaining, every single day until he was eighteen and far too big for her to manage anymore. At that point, state funding enabled him to reside at a group home not far away, where professional medical and social workers could care for his needs.

It was a hard and sorrowful blow to all of us, but especially to my mom, when Eugene died suddenly and peacefully of heart complications in his early thirties. I know she would have continued to care for him at her home, if only she could have.

My mom taught me many important lessons, including and perhaps most important that of being generous with God. She taught me by her own selfless, long-suffering life of loving sacrifice and by being the heart of our home what it means to be like the Blessed Virgin Mary, who always said yes to God.

Thank you, mom. I love you and admire you so much.

"Train up a child in the way he should,
    and when he is old he will not depart from it"
(Prv 22:6).

Chapter 49

The Crucifix

ONE OF my wife's friends, Dee, confided in her recently about a workplace situation that caused her a *lot* of aggravation. It seems Dee's co-worker Jennifer, a married Catholic woman in her thirties, was constantly rude to her. Abrasive, judgmental, and chronically contentious, Jennifer made Dee's life miserable—so much so that she eventually quit that job where she had worked for years just to get away from her. "I've got to get you out of my life" is what Dee would think each time she saw this woman.

It didn't help that Jennifer clashed with Dee on Catholic issues too. She didn't see the need to go to Mass *every* Sunday, and various other aspects of the Church also seemed optional to her. Comments like these drove Dee crazy.

What's more, Jennifer was seen as a kind of "poster girl" of success, socially and financially. She came from a prosperous and well-known local Catholic family. Her sister, who also was consistently rude to Dee, was considered one of the "pillars" of the local Catholic community. She and her husband, and kids were widely regarded as a model Catholic family, all of them popular, successful, and very active in parish life.

To complicate matters, Jennifer also happened to be a member of the parish choir Dee played piano for, so she couldn't entirely distance herself from the aggravating attitude and comments. Eventually, she couldn't take dealing with the woman there either, so she resigned from the choir.

Sharing these frustrations with her husband, Jim, Dee explained how toxic the situation had become and how she was at her wits end as to how she could deal with it. "I didn't want to quit the choir over this," she said in exasperation, "but I couldn't imagine having to be around this woman any longer! Just being in her presence makes me miserable."

Jim works full-time in law enforcement and has a small but thriving wood-working business on the side. The main thing he makes is crucifixes, large handcrafted wooden crosses with the body of Jesus affixed. One evening, as Dee was relating the latest irritating run-in she'd had with her former co-worker, Jim gently interrupted to suggest she give Jennifer one of his crucifixes.

"Impossible!" Dee laughed wryly. "First, there's no way she'd accept something like that from me, of all people, and second, I don't *like* her. Can't stand her. I don't want to be around her. Why would I want to give her a *gift*?"

Jim explained that during a recent CCD class he was teaching at the parish, the discussion had turned to a list of evil forces that can divide families. When alcoholism came up, one of the students, Jennifer's sixteen-year-old niece, spoke up emphatically, saying, "*Yes*, it sure can. I know exactly what you mean about that." That's when it clicked in Jim's mind that alcoholism might be part of the problem underlying all the drama and stress that surrounded his wife's interactions with Jennifer. "That's why I think they need a crucifix, Dee," he said.

"Fine!" she retorted. "You give it to her. I want nothing to do with it."

This struggle over whether or not to give the crucifix went on for a few weeks. Jim persisted and eventually wore Dee down. "I've been praying about this a lot," he told her. "I really feel convinced that God is telling me she needs a crucifix."

"Then *you* give it to her."

"No," he countered, "I'm not sure why, but I feel certain that God wants you to do it."

So, being the good-hearted person she is, Dee swallowed her pride and acquiesced. That following Sunday, after Mass, she approached the Jennifer's sister apprehensively, having no clue how she might react and worried that it would blow up into another fiasco, maybe even worse than the ones before. She hoped that she'd be able to just give *her* the crucifix and she would pass it along to Jennifer.

"Hey, I'd like to give you something, if you don't mind," Dee said nervously.

Eyes wide, the woman tensed up as if sensing a confrontation. "Give me something? What?"

Dee handed her a large package. "This. Jim and I think your sister should have it. Would you mind giving it to her for me?"

"What is it?" the woman said, still tense and clearly very nervous.

"Go ahead and open it," Dee smiled. "I hope you like it."

Hesitating for a moment, the woman guardedly accepted the package from Dee's outstretched hands and began to remove the wrapping paper and opened the box. When she saw the large crucifix inside, she started crying uncontrollably. Sitting down on a nearby chair, she clutched the cross to her chest and sobbed quietly, her head down. Just then, Jennifer, for whom Dee really intended the gift, noticed the commotion and stepped over to see what was happening.

Glancing down, she saw the crucifix in her sister's arms and she too, collapsed into tears, kneeling next to sister, her arms around her as they both sat there weeping for what to Dee seemed like a long time, even if it was only for a minute.

"How did you *know* we needed this?" Jennifer asked Dee plaintively, as she wiped away her tears. "How *could* you know? I always thought you hated me. I can hardly believe that you would give me a gift like . . . like *this*," she said, as her tears began to flow again. "You have no idea what a difficult and painful time I have been having, our family has been having. I've been feeling so alone and scared. And you . . ." she trailed off.

"Jim and I wanted you to have this," Dee said quietly, shocked by the transformation, "because we realized that something was wrong and you must be hurting, and we just want you to know that Jesus loves you and can help you and your family get through whatever it is that's challenging you right now."

And then, the most amazing thing happened. All the anger and acrimony between the two of them simply evaporated. It suddenly vanished. And a kind of friendship began to grow where before there had only been thorns and broken glass. Truly a miracle of God's healing grace, if you ask me. I don't know the ways in which God is working in Jennifer's life and that of her family. Nor does Dee, but she has seen with her own eyes the power of the Cross of Christ, a power so strong and so deep that even the most stubborn animosities and divisions are unable to withstand it. It's the power of love. God's love.

Post Script: When Dee first told me this story, I thought of the words of the famous Simon and Garfunkel song "Bridge Over Troubled Water." I think this part perfectly summarizes the lesson here—how Jesus Christ will heal and help us, if we will only let him:

When you're weary, feeling small,
When tears are in your eyes, I will dry them all;
I'm on your side. When times get rough
And friends just can't be found,
Like a bridge over troubled water
I will lay me down.
Like a bridge over troubled water
I will lay me down.

When you're down and out,
When you're on the street,
When evening falls so hard
I will comfort you.
I'll take your part.
When darkness comes
And pain is all around,
Like a bridge over troubled water
I will lay me down.
Like a bridge over troubled water
I will lay me down.

———————◆———————

"Brethren, if a man is overtaken in any trespass, you who are spiritual should restore him in a spirit of gentleness. Look to yourself, lest you too be tempted. Bear one another's burdens, and so fulfil the law of Christ" (Gal 6:1–2).

"There is no fear in love, but perfect love casts out fear. For fear has to do with punishment, and he who fears is

*not perfected in love. We love, because he first loved us.
If anyone says, 'I love God,' and hates his brother, he is
a liar; for he who does not love his brother whom he has
seen, cannot love God whom he has not seen. And this
commandment we have from him, that he who loves God
should love his brother also"* (1 Jn 4:18-21).

*"If I speak in the tongues of men and of angels, but have
not love, I am a noisy gong or a clanging cymbal. And if
I have prophetic powers, and understand all mysteries
and all knowledge, and if I have all faith, so as to remove
mountains, but have not love, I am nothing. If I give
away all I have, and if I deliver my body to be burned,
but have not love, I gain nothing.*

*Love is patient and kind; love is not jealous or boastful;
it is not arrogant or rude. Love does not insist on its own
way; it is not irritable or resentful; it does not rejoice at
wrong, but rejoices in the right. Love bears all things,
believes all things, hopes all things, endures all things.*

*Love never ends. . . . So faith, hope, love abide, these
three; but the greatest of these is love"* (1 Cor 13:1-8, 13).

Chapter 50

The Hourglass

THEY SAY every good story must come to an end. This is true, of course, for any story we human beings can tell, whether fact or fiction. All the stories I've told you in the preceding pages of this book are true; they happened to me or, in one or two instances, to people who've told me personally the details of what happened. But these fifty true stories are, like all works of man, finite and final.

Not so, however, for another kind of story—the one that continues from here to eternity. That kind of story is, as St. Thérèse of Lisieux's biography is beautifully and simply titled, *the story of a soul*. It has a beginning, once upon a time, but will never end because the good God who created us and everything else out of pure love has an eternity of happiness waiting for those who love him and seek him with all their heart, mind, and strength.

> For God so loved the world that he gave his only-begotten Son, that whoever believes in him should not perish but have eternal life. (Jn 3:16)

Even those who, tragically, refuse God's love and die unrepentant in that state (the Bible calls that horrifying condition "mortal sin" [*cf.* 1 John 5:16–17]), will continue to exist for all eternity, though separated forever from the God who loves them but who also respects their freedom to say "no" to him.

The most important lesson I've learned in life is the value of time. It's precious beyond measure because it's irretrievable once it runs out. The image of an hourglass helps me contemplate the preciousness of time, each second of which is like a grain of sand passing from the top to the bottom, never to return, never to be repeated.

A long time ago, I wrote a little reflection called "How I Pray Now,"[1] in which I consider the significance and time, especially given how much of it I've wasted in my life:

> I find that my mental prayer at the end of the day is when I am best able to focus my mind and heart. I survey the day and its contents and speak to the Lord about how I think it went. And I ask Him how He thinks it went: "I know you've given me a limited number of days on this earth, Lord. Please help me make the best use of them I can." Time is what I pray about most. The older I get, the more I appreciate the preciousness of time. I only have so much of it allotted to me, and there are no reruns. I have to be busy attending to my Father's work before the sand in my particular hourglass runs out. So, Lord please keep me focused.

It's weird. The truth that our own individual hourglass of life contains only so many grains of sand is something we all know—in other words, our mortality is real. At some point, sooner or later, each of us will die and depart this earthly life for the eternal life to come. And yet most of us (I have been guilty of this often enough) tend to ignore this reality, assuming we have plenty of life ahead. "I'll get around to that *someday*" we tell ourselves. "There's plenty of time to fix that,

---

[1] It appears as a chapter in my book *Envoy for Christ: 25 Years as a Catholic Apologist* (Cincinnati: Servant Books, 2012)

or reconcile with him, or repair the damage I did there," we rationalize. "Sure, I want to be holy! And eventually I will because, hey, there's plenty of time for that down the road, but I'm not quite ready yet."

Terms like "eventually," "someday," and "in the future" are like little drips and drops of self-administered anesthesia, dulling the sense of urgency we should all have when it comes to making the most of our opportunities to live a life pleasing to God so that we'll be ready when the time comes to offer it all back to him, for better or for worse.

Time in this life is like wet cement. Because it hasn't set yet, it's still malleable. You can shape it, mold it, and make handprints in it. But when the cement dries and hardens, you can no longer change it. Passing from time into eternity, when that last grain of sand falls from the top of the hourglass of your life into the bottom (Heaven or Hell for all eternity), the opportunity to change, forgive, repent, etc. will have passed you by forever. So you have to ask yourself one question: Do you feel lucky?

Providentially, luck as nothing to do with it. "Take delight in the LORD," Scripture says, "and he will give you the desires of your heart. Commit your way to the LORD; trust in him, and he will act. He will bring forth your vindication as the light, and your right as the noonday" (Ps 37:4–6).

"Woulda, coulda, shoulda." Isn't it true that many people find themselves saying those words near the end of their lives as they look back and survey all the lost opportunities they let slip away to be good, loving, forgiving, compassionate, faithful, honorable, selfless, and kind? But by then, it's too late.

That haunting line from has-been prizefighter in *On the Waterfront* reminds me of those who let their lives slip by without making the most of it for God's sake and then find themselves forever separated from the winner's circle in Heaven: "I could've had class. I could have been a contender. I could've been somebody, instead of a bum, which is what I am. Let's face it."

Now, if I've learned anything in these first fifty years, I've learned that I absolutely do *not* want to reach the end of my earthly life—the end of Part I of my own personal never-ending story—filled with regrets for what I woulda, coulda, and shoulda done in response to God's love. Rather, I want to be ready for the day the Lord calls me to come unto him.

I want him to find me, when the time comes, not like Adam in the Garden, naked and afraid, fearful of the punishment that awaits but rather loving him and loving others for his sake, whatever form the latter might take. Imperfectly, yes, for surely everything I've done in my life has been *at best* imperfect, much of it far worse. But I'm learning! I'm learning how precious time is, how quickly it goes by, and how little we value it until it's gone. And how much I can do with it, or rather, how much God can do with it in me, if only I allow it. Everything else is just bits of fluff and flotsam flying away from me in the winds of time. Or as St. Teresa of Avila put it:

> Let nothing disturb you,
> Let nothing frighten you,
> All things are passing away:
> God never changes.
> Patience obtains all things
> Whoever has God lacks nothing;
> God alone suffices.

This, then, is the final lesson, both in terms of this book and of this earthly life. Even if you and I learn all the other lessons I've mentioned here, and a million more besides, none of it will matter if we don't learn *and live* the lesson of the hourglass. The sand of time is running out, little by little. In due time, sooner or later, this earthly life will end and we will have to give an account of our lives to God. But this is nothing to fear, for those who love him. It is, rather, the cause of our joy for it means that one day will be graduation day! School's out forever! Endless summer! And you will be happy with God and his angels and saints forever in Heaven. That's the glorious Part II of the never-ending story.

───────────◆───────────

"*Therefore it is said,*
  '*Awake, O sleeper, and arise from the dead,*
  and Christ shall give you light.'
Look carefully then how you walk, not as unwise men but as wise, making the most of the time, because the days are evil. Therefore, do not be foolish, but understand what the will of the Lord is" (Eph 5:14–17).

"*It is appointed for men to die once, and after that comes judgment*" (Heb 9:27).

"*Come now, you who say, 'Today or tomorrow we will go into such and such a town and spend a year there and trade and get gain'; whereas you do not know about tomorrow. What is your life? For you are a mist that appears for a little time and then vanishes. Instead you ought to say, 'If the Lord wills, we shall live and we shall do this or that'*" (Jas 4:13–15).

"*And some one said to him, 'Lord, will those who are saved be few?' And he said to them, 'Strive to enter by the narrow door; for many, I tell you, will seek to enter and will not be able. When once the householder has risen up and shut the door, you will begin to stand outside and to knock at the door, saying, "Lord, open to us." He will answer you, "I do not know where you come from." Then you will begin to say, "We ate and drank in your presence, and you taught in our streets." But he will say, "I tell you, I do not know where you come from; depart from me, all you workers of iniquity!" There you will weep and gnash your teeth, when you see Abraham and Isaac and Jacob and all the prophets in the kingdom of God and you yourselves thrust out'"* (Lk 13:23–28).

"Besides this you know what hour it is, how it is full time now for you to wake from sleep. For salvation is nearer to us now than when we first believed; the night is far gone, the day is at hand. Let us then cast off the works of darkness and put on the armor of light; let us conduct ourselves becomingly as in the day, not in reveling and drunkenness, not in debauchery and licentiousness, not in quarreling and jealousy. But put on the Lord Jesus Christ, and make no provision for the flesh, to gratify its desires" (Rom 13:11–14).

About the Author

PATRICK MADRID is a life-long Catholic. He hosts the popular daily "Patrick Madrid Show" on Immaculate Heart Radio (Monday–Friday, 6–9 a.m. Pacific) and, before launching that show, hosted the show "Right Here, Right Now," broadcast on approximately 300 AM and FM stations across the U.S., as well as on Sirius Satellite Radio and globally via shortwave. He is also a frequent guest and occasional guest-host on the "Catholic Answers Live" radio program.

Patrick has authored or edited twenty-four books on Catholic themes, including *Why Be Catholic? Search and Rescue, Does the Bible Really Say That?* and the acclaimed *Surprised by Truth* series.

Commenting publicly on the effectiveness of Patrick's approach to doing apologetics, Cardinal Edward Egan, Archbishop Emeritus of New York, said, *"How do you bring a friend or relative back into the Church? First you pray. Then, you follow Patrick Madrid's advice in [his book]* Search and Rescue."

Patrick worked at Catholic Answers for eight years, where he served as vice president. A veteran of a dozen formal, public debates with Protestant ministers, Mormon leaders, and other non-Catholic spokesmen, Patrick has presented countless seminars on Catholic themes, in English and Spanish, at parishes, universities, and conferences across the United States and around the world.

For nearly thirty years, Patrick has published numerous popular articles on Scripture, Church history, patristics, apologetics, and evangelization in various Catholic and Protestant periodicals, and he has contributed scholarly articles on apologetics in the *New Catholic Encyclopedia*.

He earned a Bachelor of Science degree in business at the University of Phoenix, as well as a Bachelor of Philosophy in philosophy and a Masters of Arts in dogmatic theology at the Pontifical College Josephinum (Columbus, OH). He is currently pursuing a doctorate in Church history.

Patrick has served as an adjunct professor of theology at Franciscan University of Steubenville and currently teaches as an adjunct professor of theology in the graduate theology program at Holy Apostles College and Seminary in Cromwell, Connecticut.

Married for thirty-five years, Patrick and his wife Nancy have been blessed by the Lord with eleven children and eighteen grandchildren (so far).

Patrick's website is patrickmadrid.com.